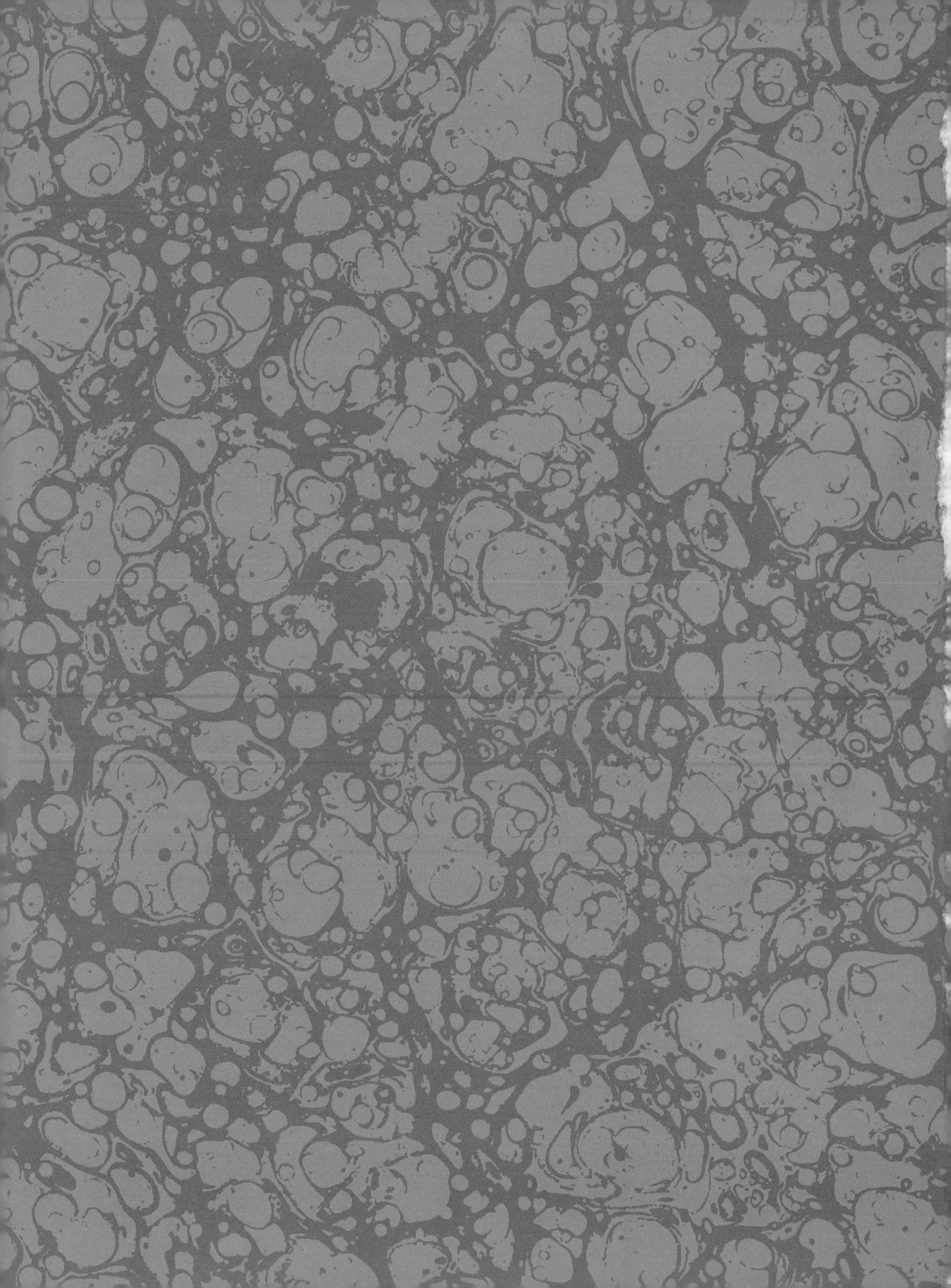

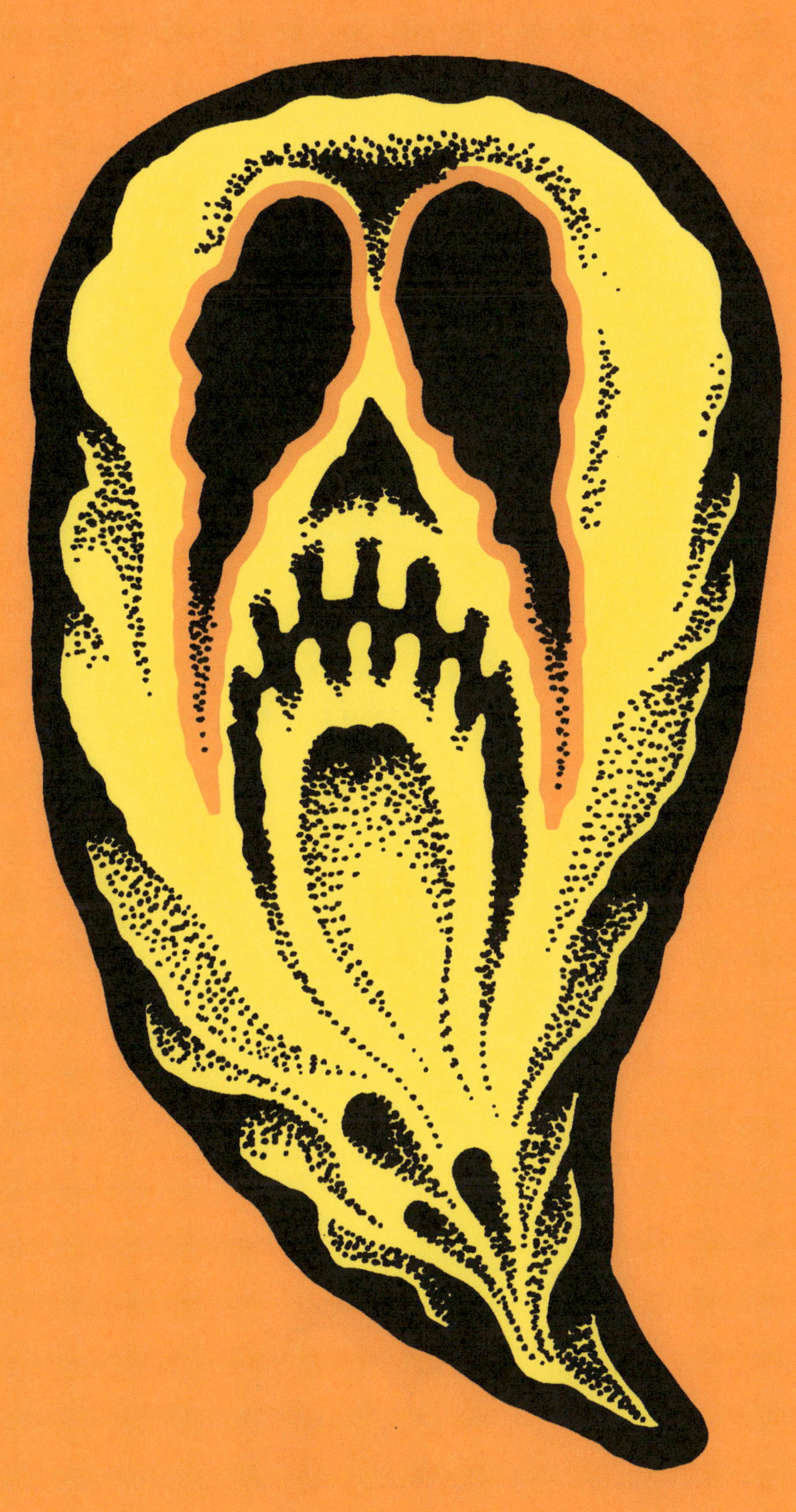

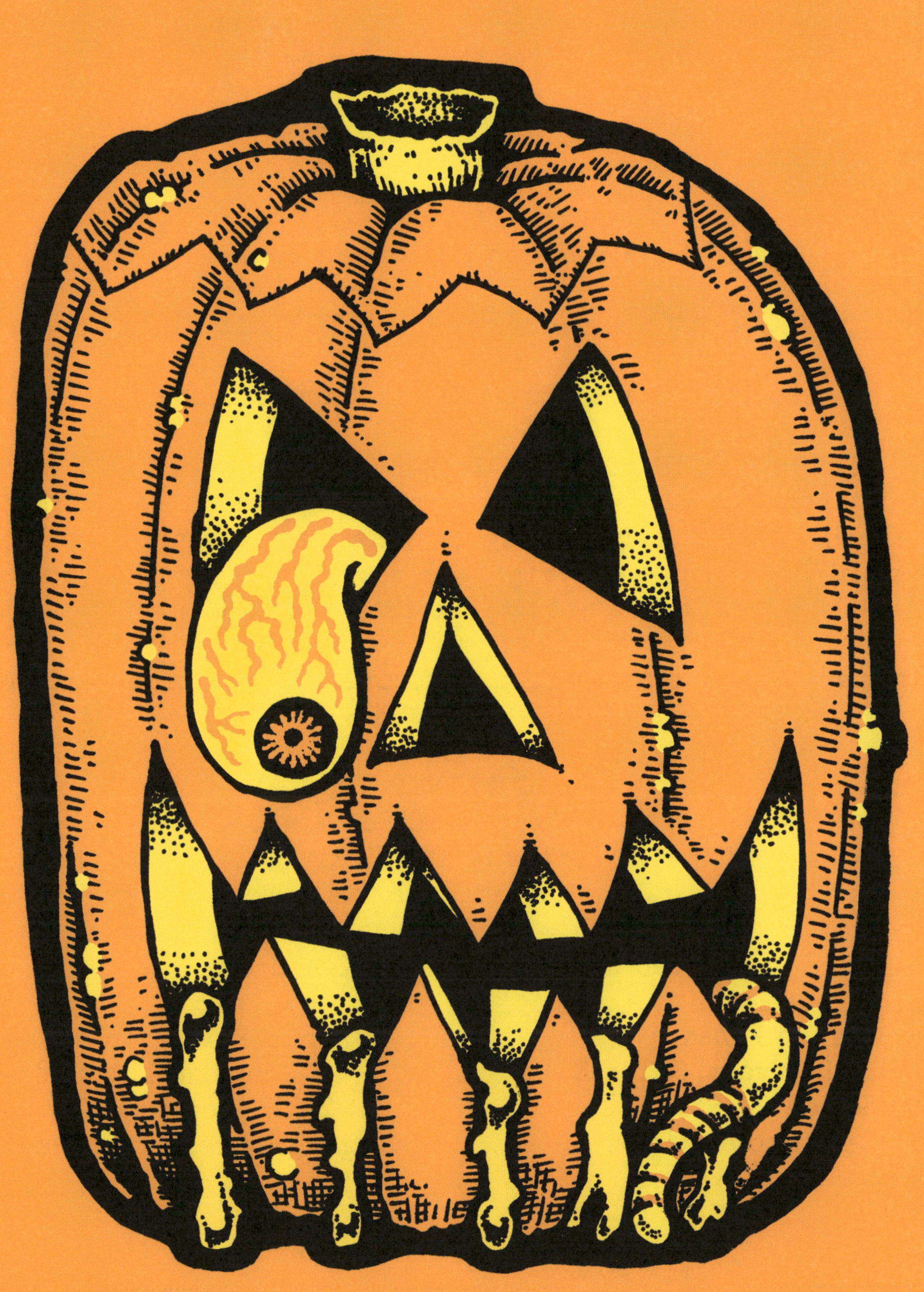

Sean Äaberg's
Halloween Book

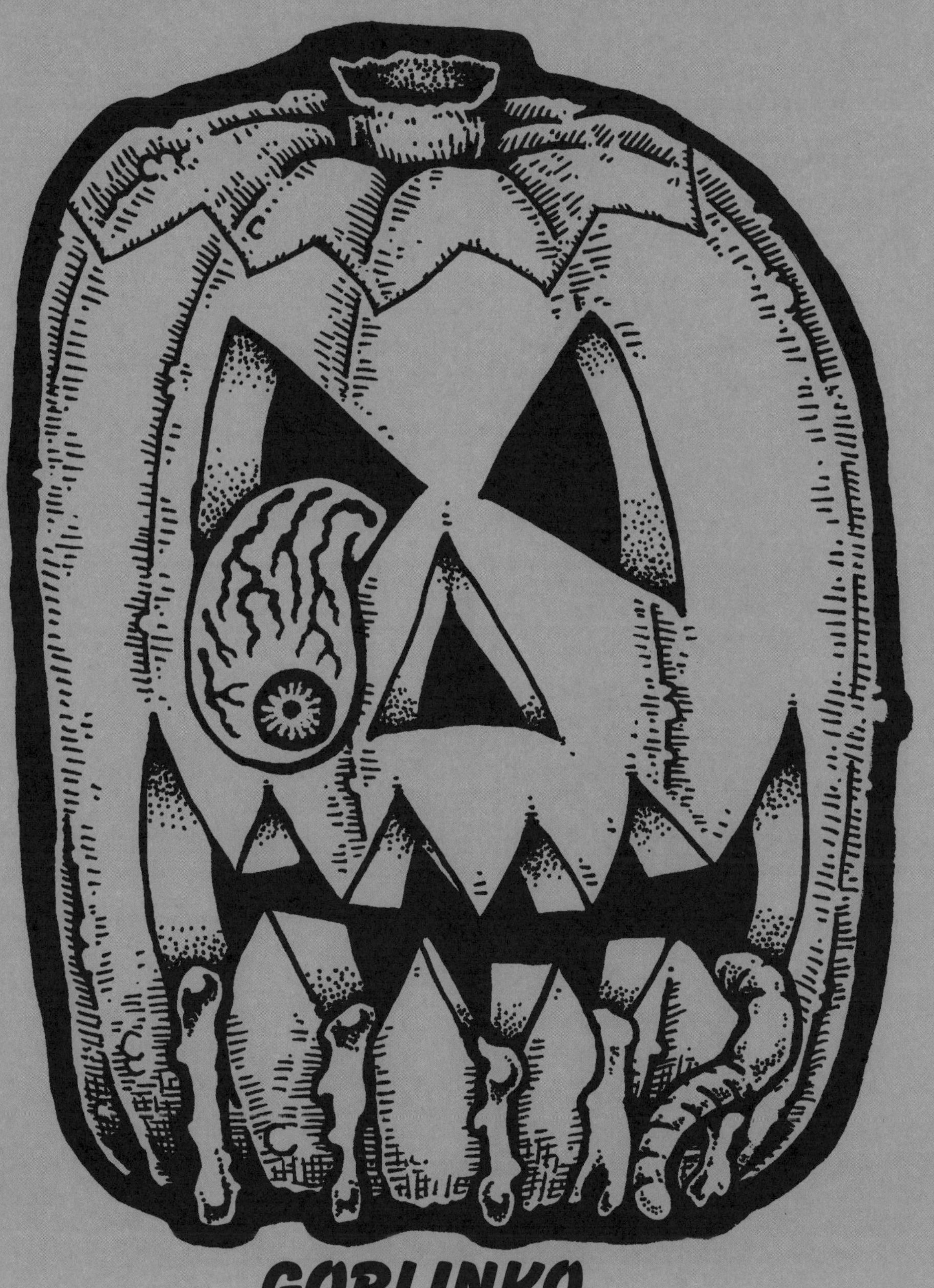

GOBLINKO

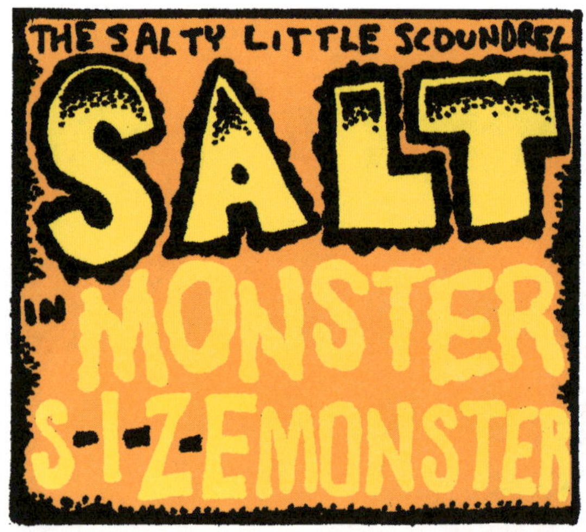

THE SALTY LITTLE SCOUNDREL
SALT
IN MONSTER
S-I-Z-E MONSTER

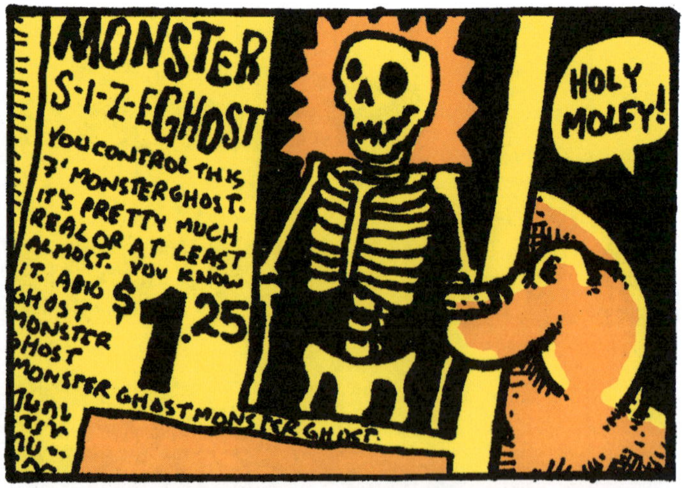

MONSTER
S-I-Z-E GHOST
YOU CONTROL THIS
7' MONSTER GHOST.
IT'S PRETTY MUCH
REAL OR AT LEAST
ALMOST. YOU KNOW
IT. A BIG $1.25
GHOST
MONSTER
GHOST
MONSTER GHOST MONSTER GHOST.
HOLY MOLEY!

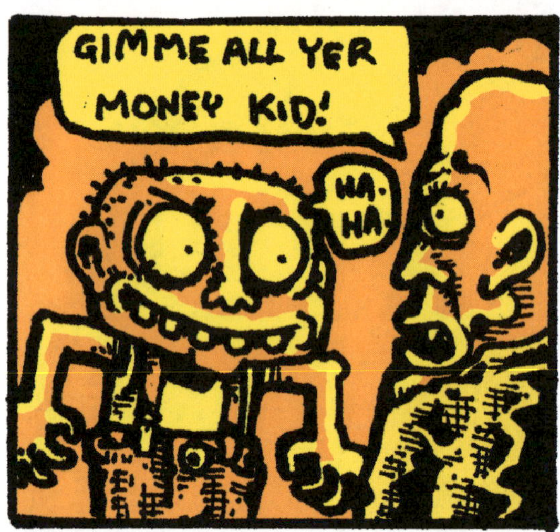

GIMME ALL YER MONEY KID!
HA HA

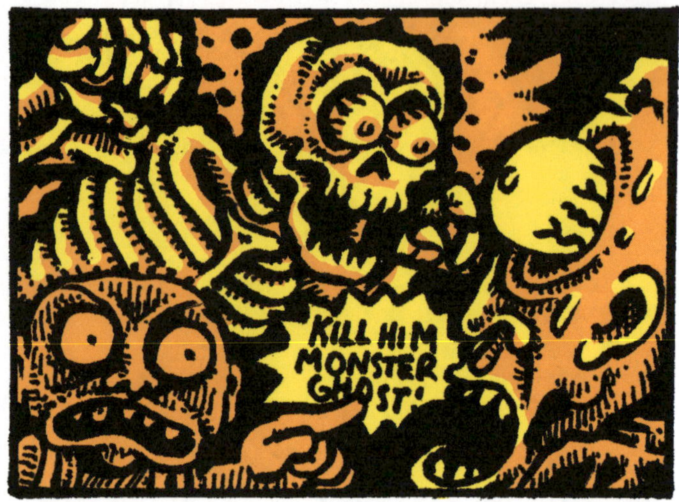

KILL HIM MONSTER GHOST!

7 FEET TALL
IN AUTHENTIC
COLORS WITH
GLOW IN THE
DARK EYES!
YOUR MONEY
BACK IF NOT
SATISFACTORILY
HORRIFIED!

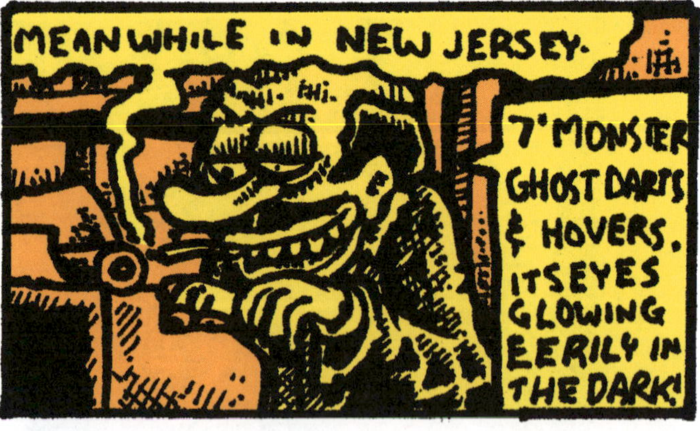

MEANWHILE IN NEW JERSEY.
HI. HI.
7' MONSTER
GHOST DARTS
& HOVERS.
ITS EYES
GLOWING
EERILY IN
THE DARK!

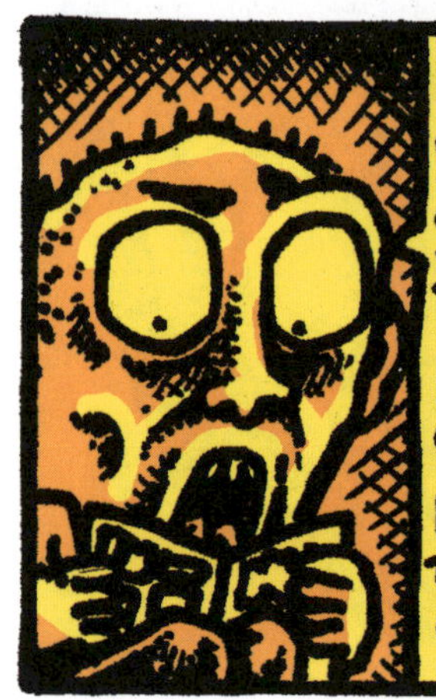

WAIT! X-RAY
SPECS! WOW!
SCIENTIFIC OP-
TICAL PRINCIPLE
REALLY WORKS
YOU SEEM TO
BE ABLE TO SEE
THROUGH FLESH
AND SEE THE
BONES BENEATH!

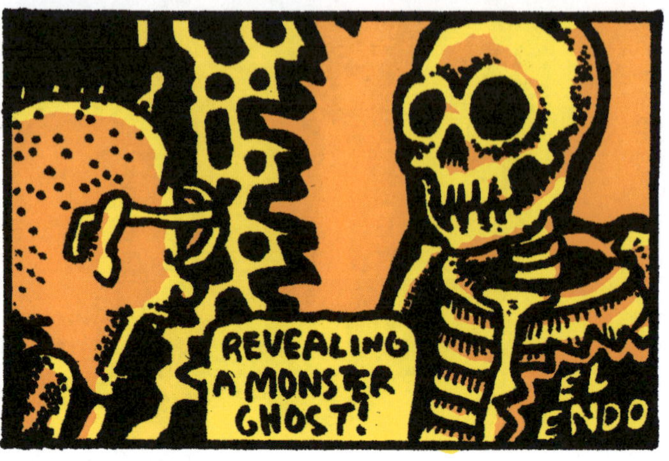

REVEALING
A MONSTER
GHOST!
EL ENDO

Introduction

I've always loved Halloween. Something deep in the core of my being resonates with the holiday. On a superficial level I love the costumes, the candy, the colors & the general spooky & corny vibe, on a deeper level, the more I learn about Halloween & the more context it gains in my brain, the more I love it. It's like a picture coming into clearer & clearer resolution. I would spend all year as a kid drawing Jack O'Lanterns, witches & other Halloween things, not so much as a preparation for, but as a way of reminding myself of the comfort I felt on Halloween. I liked that everyone let their Freak Flag fly on Halloween even if, as an adult, I didn't think they were doing it right. Society has always been buttoned up & dishonest, but on Halloween it's a time to be real & disrupt the status quo. I love this freedom & disruption & especially that it is a holiday for kids. While I have my own kids now & can basically do what I want, I want to share my love & vision of Halloween with you.

xox Sean Äaberg
Portland, Oregon.
October 2021

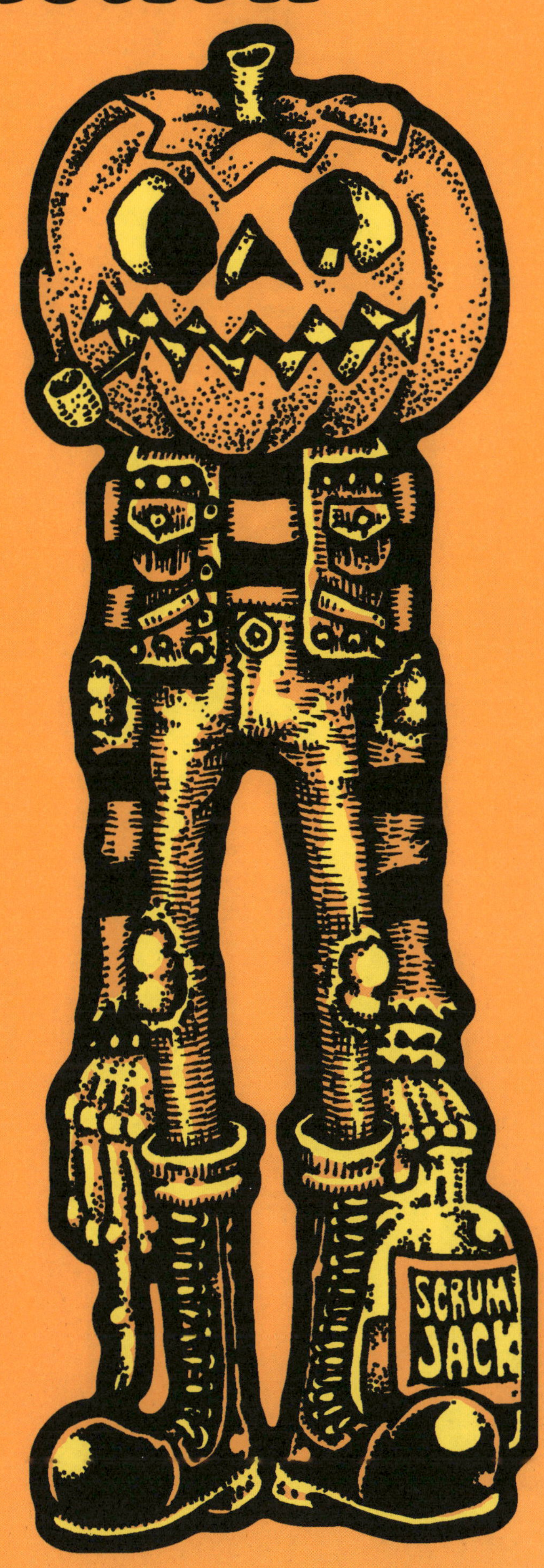

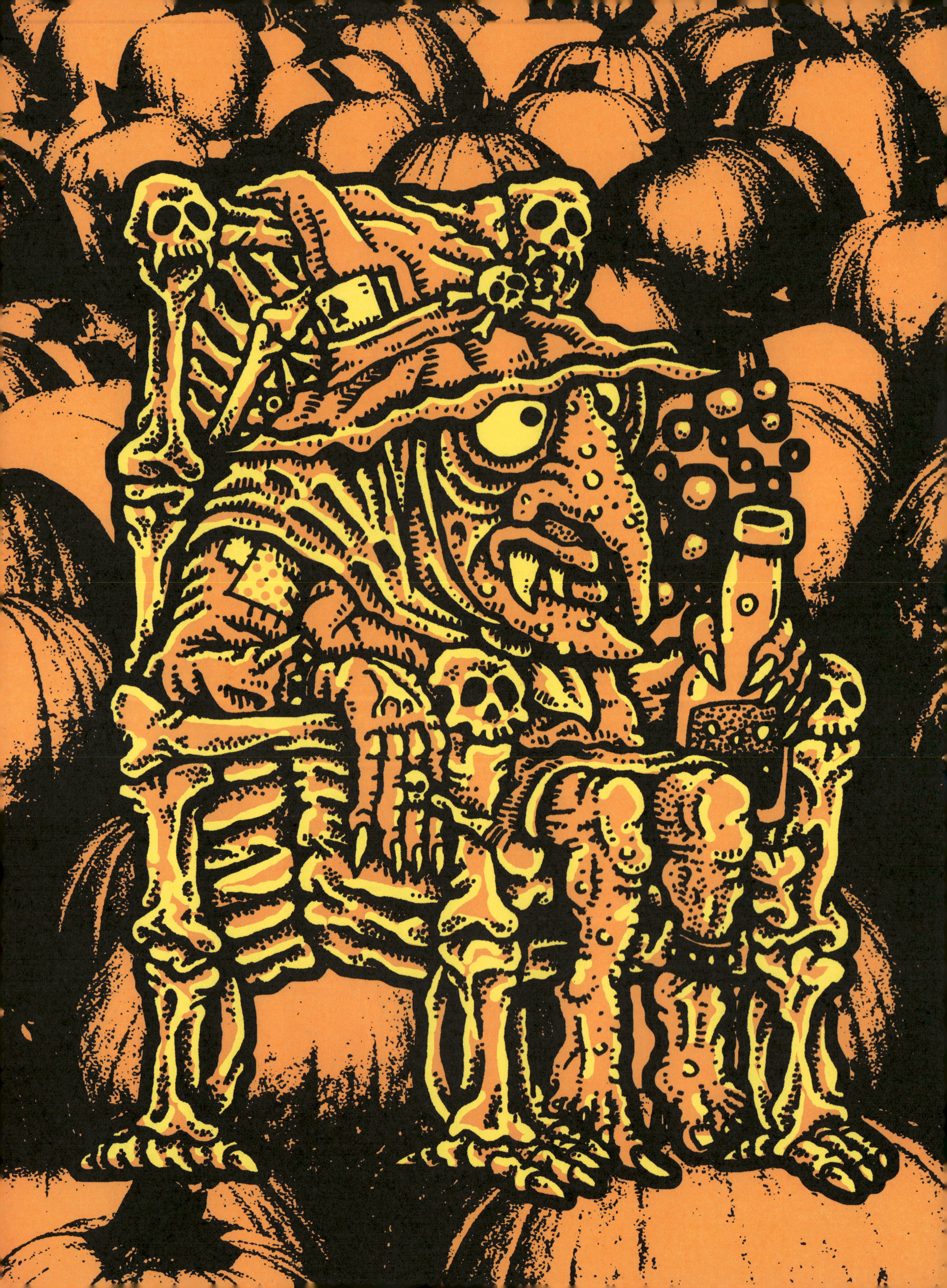

Table of Contents

Halloween Today

"If ever there was a holiday that deserves to be commercialized, it's Halloween. We haven't taken it away from kids. We've just expanded it so that the kid in adults can enjoy it, too."

- Cassandra Peterson aka Elvira

Halloween today lives on in people's hearts & everyone has their own way of celebrating the holiday. The Halloween displays come out earlier & earlier without the familial stress & depression that Christmas can evoke. People are generally stoked & inspired by the early arrival of the Halloween aisle. There isn't some kind of "What Halloween Is" agreement from the people although everyone knows Halloween when they see it. Aside from my love of the holiday, "What Halloween Is" is partly what this book is about. Having the market guide a holiday is good for some things like gauging how popular a thing is & letting it evolve quickly, on the other hand it's terrible for things like clarity of vision & tradition. I think a combination of both open-market & some kind of direction or control is what works best. Because it's good to let people decide what they like but it's also important to have some kind of organization to direct how things go. You need both. That said, Halloween is by nature Anarchic, so trying to direct it is a fool's errand. I figure that I already live in Portland & the USA which are similarly uncontrollable, so I need to figure out a way to guide this thing however I can, by any means necessary or as I say "anything goes" or in the case of

Halloween we're going to go with "Trick or Treat". By presenting my vision of Halloween as a treat, I hope you will be inspired to do Halloween proper!

I am naturally attracted to history & tradition in a way that most people aren't, so part of my job in life is to get people to be interested in history & tradition in a similar way. My basic argument for history is that it gives things context that they lack otherwise. If you know the story behind things they expand in meaning & depth in a way that ordinary familiarity doesn't compare to. When you understand the story behind things, they start to interlock & grow into one another. Life becomes more dimensional, meaningful & fun in a way that animalistic ignorance can't compare to.

Halloween means different things to different people. The two main, contradictory thrusts are that it means "Be Yourself" to the people that feel like they fit in better to the Halloween world & "Be Something You're Not" to the people who fit in better to the non-Halloween world. I am writing to both camps in this book. I feel like I've been in the fitting in to Halloween Camp my whole life but I recognize the need for definition, restraint & the like. Because of these contradictory elements, I'm sensitive to the idea of Halloween feeling like the day when you get to "be yourself", but I'd argue that you & society would be a lot healthier if you would "be yourself" every day.

Tradition is a bulwark against the chaos in this world that is always threatening to destroy everything that we build. Tradition is cultural continuity. I am a child of divorce & I grew up in the chaotic city of Oakland, California, in the post-1960s tumult so I am attracted to tradition out of necessity! I also am used to chaos. While I appreciate that chaos can dissolve the rigidity & corruption of order, when the scales are unbalanced, there are consequences down the line, these consequences were made abundantly clear when I was a child. Anyhow, I drag my own package of traditions with me & I feel like I need to share them with the people because the traditions are yearning to carry on outside of the confines of my family. As the world has gotten increasingly chaotic, tradition has increased in value to a level that we haven't seen previously. So, in a world of shifting sands, tradition is a concrete structure of repetition! Every time a tradition is repeated it grows in strength & more of these shifting sands are held down by the cultural roots that we are laying down.

Halloween Yesterday

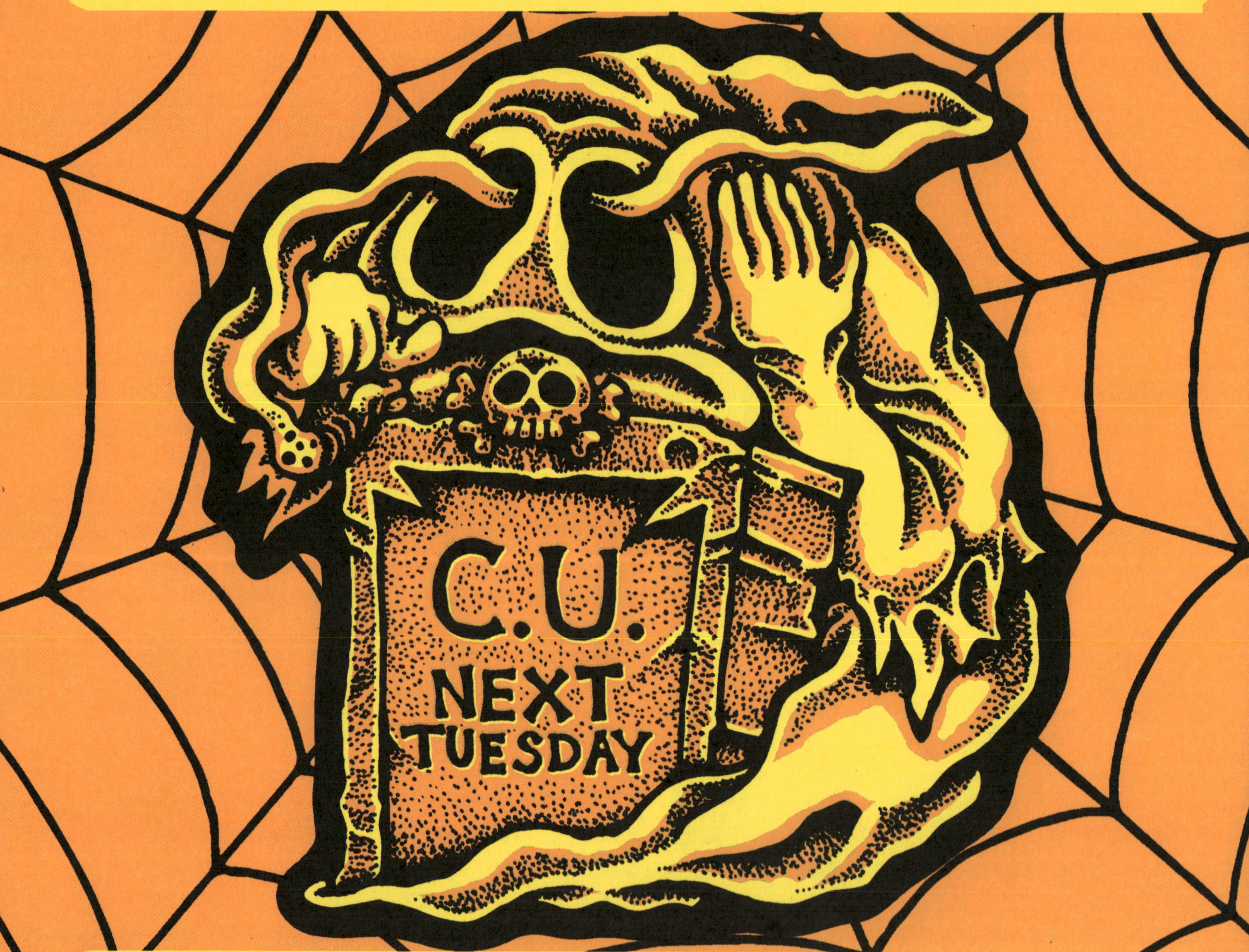

Halloween originally came from Ireland & the surrounding areas & made its way to the United States in the crumb-filled pockets & brains of Irish immigrants trying to make a better life for themselves. The holiday was tinged with the Germanic love/fear of demons, devils, witches & monsters & mixed with mercantilism & childishness in the ghettoes of America's East Coast to become what it became. As time passes Halloween becomes what we know it as & the passing of trends & the history of Halloween, while important are less important than what the actuality of Halloween is now.

The natural world that humanity came out of is drastically different than the human defined one in which we find ourselves. What we're gonna do right here is go back, way back, back into time, back thousands of years. We used to be at the mercy of nature in a way that most of us would find incomprehensible. In this world of natural primacy, the way of perceiving things was based on nature, first & foremost. So, the big, important characters in people's lives were forces of nature like the Sun, Moon & the passage of time through the seasons. The wind & the rain & the snow meant a lot more, they meant survival. The world was peppered with near-monsters like wolves, bears, eagles & the like that wouldn't just kill you, they would compete with you for food. Life was short, brutal & harsh. People would be considered old in their forties & lose their teeth before that. It was in this world that the Pagan roots of Halloween & the other major holidays first developed. Extra sensitive people could sense that the period from late October into early November was very different than the other times of year.

As humanity got a foothold & slowly mastered nature, the natural world gave way to a more self-defined world. As humans started to cultivate crops, culture started to develop. As soon as culture developed it started to snowball in its complexity & Halloween went from being defined by nature to being defined by humanity. So the natural world observations of the extra-sensitive humans (you can call them Shamans) informed the culture of the people who followed them & eventually we have something that resembles the Halloween that we celebrate today! Halloween comes from the Irish in particular, but most cultures in the world have a celebration at a similar time & manner. It's with all of this that we go into this exploration of Halloween. It's particularly important to bring in an evolutionary angle because these sorts of considerations give a weight & universality to the discussion.

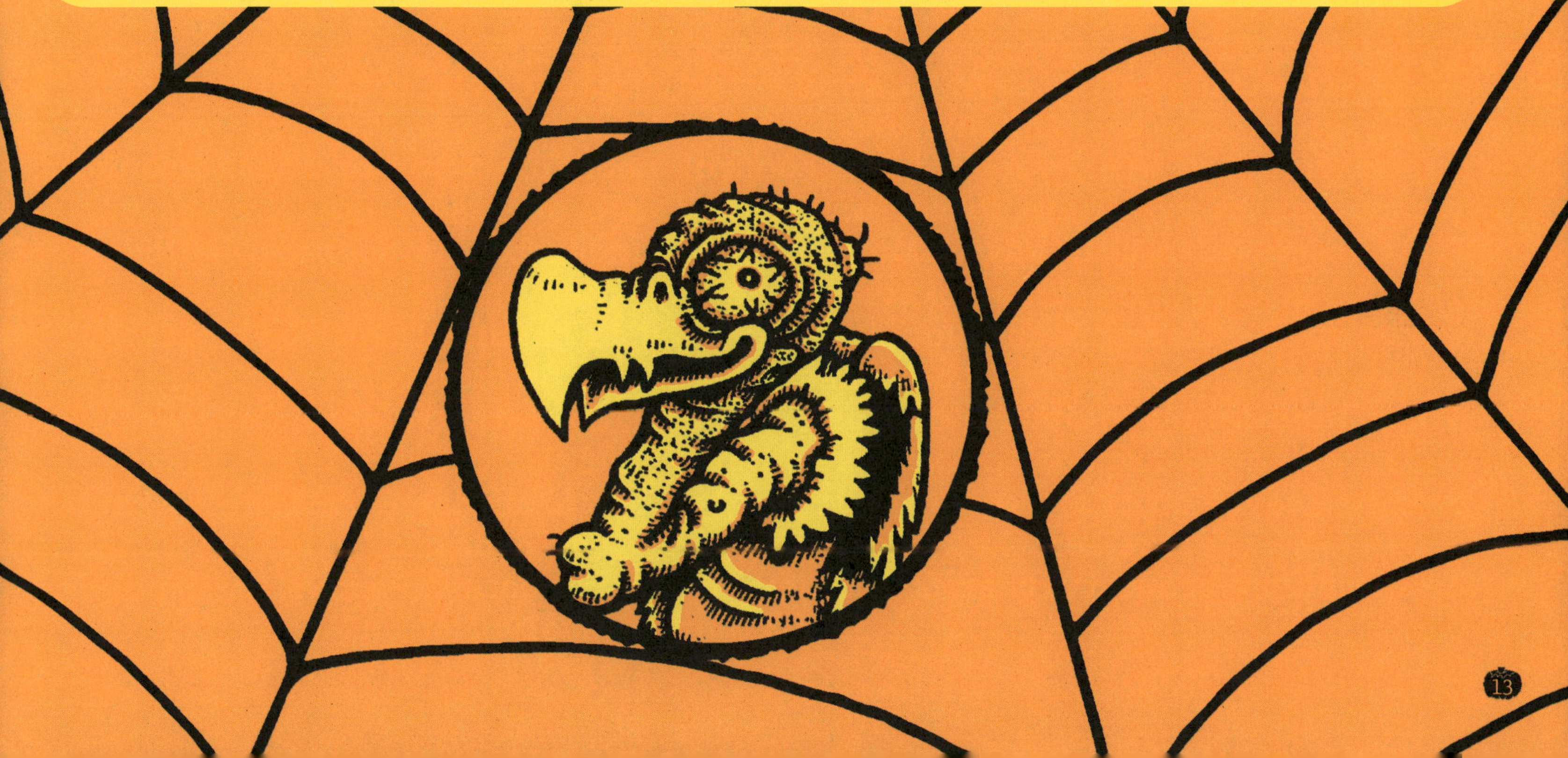

Old Halloween Traditions

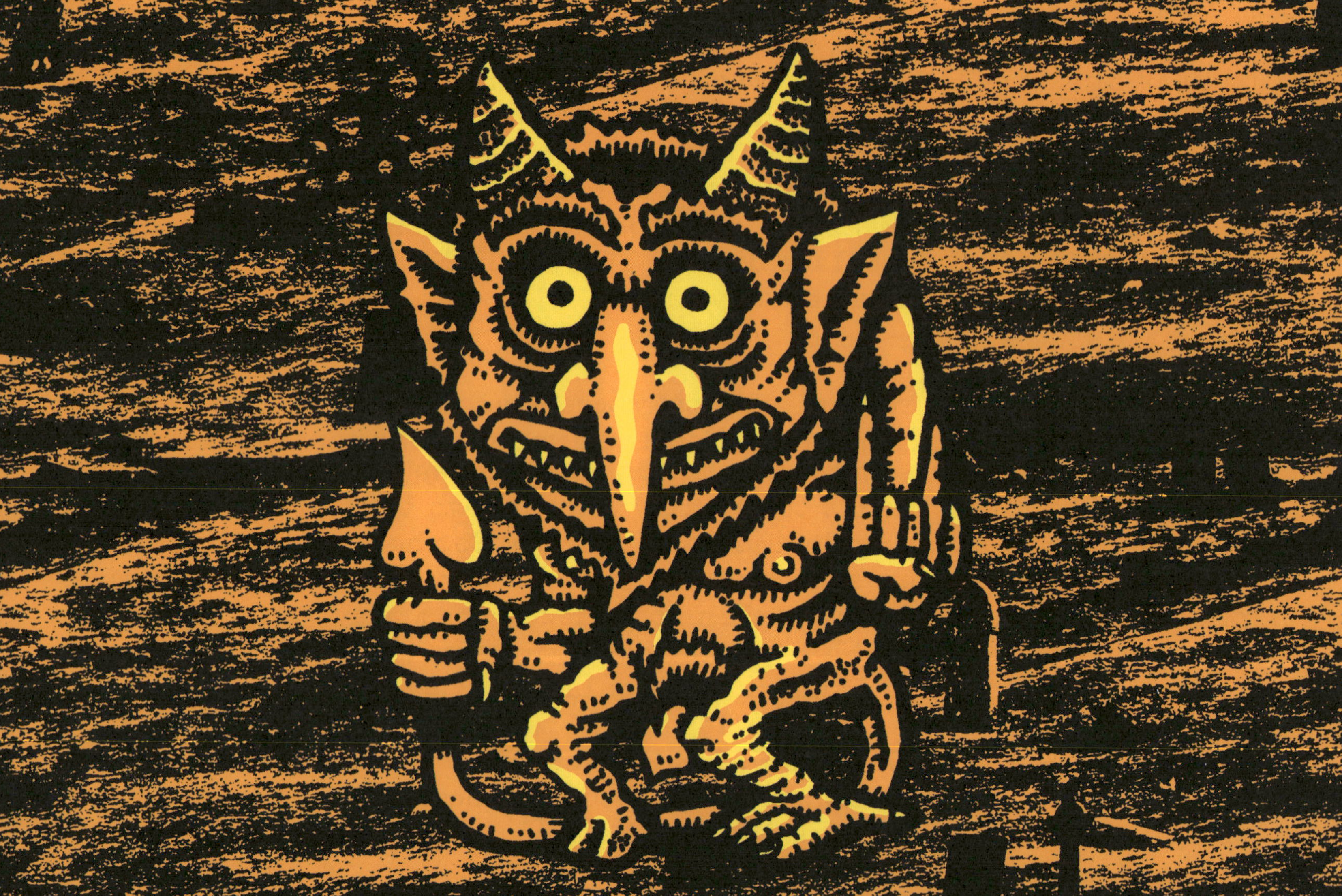

Halloween must be seen as an atavistic tendency: a seasonal resurgence of something ancient & pagan. It doesn't need to be viewed as oppositional to whatever societal control mechanism you or those around you subscribe to, but is better understood as a necessary steam release. If it is not seen this way, Halloween is misunderstood & society explodes. The old belief is that Halloween is the day when the veil between the world of the living & the world of the dead is thinnest. A time which coincides with the harvest, the transition from the summer into the winter & the land is drying out & things are dying. Spiders are spinning their webs, the smoke from wildfires is coloring the sky, the sun & the moon orange, leaves on the trees are turning yellow & orange & falling to the ground. We prepare for the dead part of the year & death is on our minds. As humanity grows further & further from our roots, it grows in importance to recognize the natural traditions we evolved with.

Long before Christianity made its way through Europe, the people were Pagan, that is, their spiritual observations came from their relationship with the Earth. Whatever tribal group these peoples belonged to determined the specifics of their beliefs, but it is most important to not view these ways in a Christian context. So, people observed the passage of time & the position of the Earth in space & how these things effected reality & these were their ways. I hesitate to use the word "beliefs" even because I feel like it is more of a relationship. Anyhow, it is in these relationships between humans & the Earth that the roots of Halloween are found in old prehistoric traditions.

It is safe to assume that most of the Halloween traditions start with the Gaelic festival of Samhain. Samhain happens on November 1st (using the Gregorian calendar) & marks the end of the lighter part of the year & brings on the dark part of the year. Samhain coincides with the end of harvest, so there is animal slaughtering & the adding of animal blood to the fields, bonfires, drinking, a celebration of life & the death that sustains it! It was believed that the doors to the world of the dead were open because of the weird feeling in the air.

This world of prehistoric Paganism gave way to the traditions of the new Europe which had an overlay of Imperial Rome & eventually that overlay became Roman Catholic. Out of this new mix came Mumming & Guising, progenitors of Trick or Treating. With Mumming groups of people act in traditional skits on the street for treats & with Guising groups of people dress up, usually with masks & go door to door doing skits for treats. Guising occurred on holidays other than Samhain & still happens on Christmas. These have changed into Trick or Treating where the giving of treats comes with a threat of a trick, but the trick part of Halloween has lessened over time.

Divination is also a popular Samhain activity which has passed on to Halloween. The doors to the land of the dead being open, it is easier to contact otherworldly entities, including the dead themselves! The people would use readily available Fall apples & nuts for divination.

An older name for Halloween was "Snap Apple Night". The night was a big party & people would specifically bob for apples in a tub of water or try to bite apples suspended from strings. Divination was also popular, including a method of reading apple peels. Apples would be fully in season & people would be making games out of anything they could get their hands on. "When life gives you apples…"

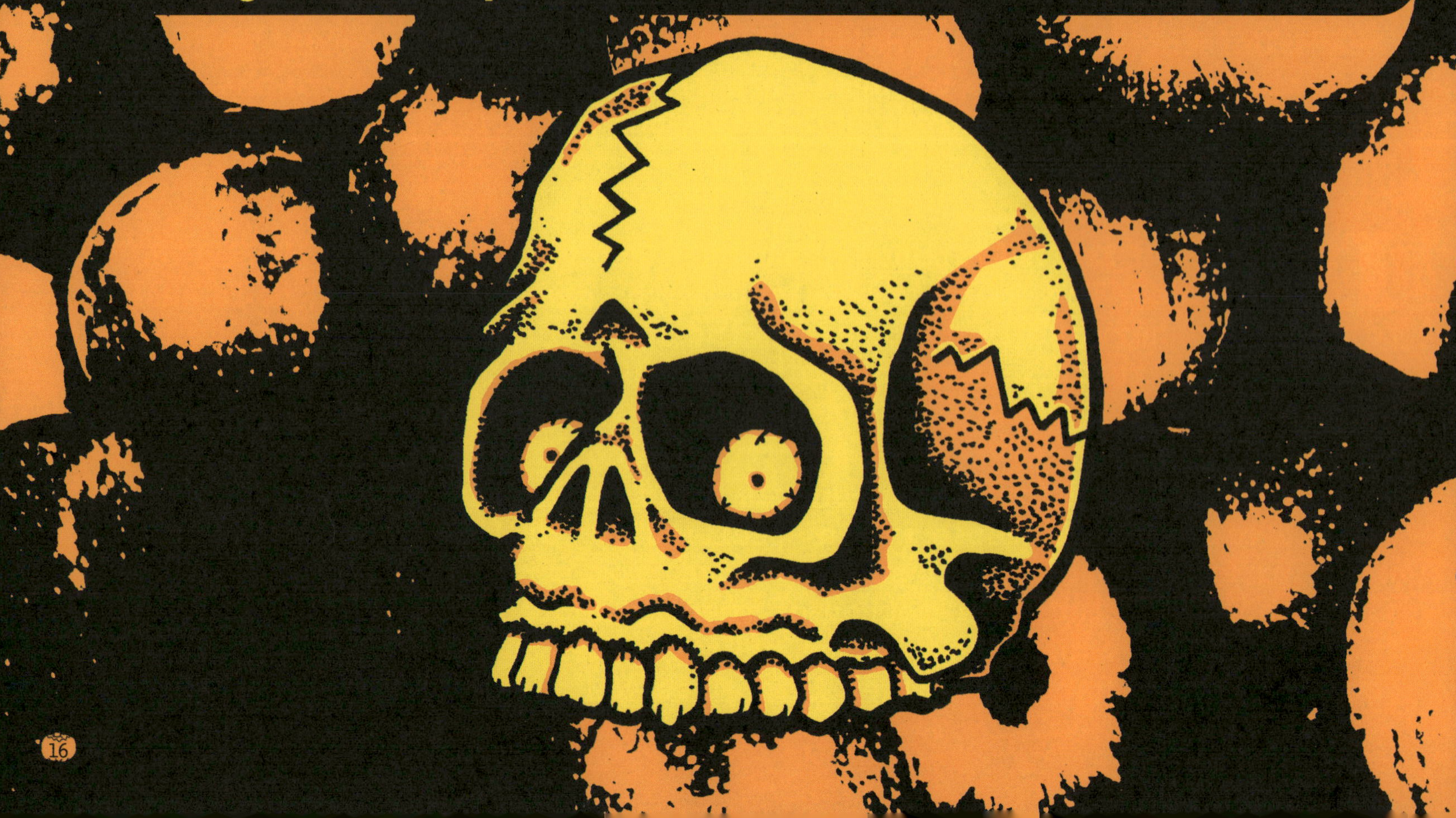

While the Pagan origins of Halloween are fun you cannot deny the Christian contributions to the holiday & its spread before its total secularization. Christianity spread throughout the world as part of the Roman Empire, dominating Europe from 400 AD to 1806 AD. The Roman Catholic Empire served to unite the tribes of Europe under one belief system & absorbed old Pagan beliefs into it & spread them around in a way that would be impossible for the disparate Pagan tribes previous. Remnants of Pagan Europe still linger all over the place, but this was part of the Roman Catholic Empire's strategy. As Catholicism spread over the globe, they effectively used one coat of thin paint on their new converts allowing their real colors to shine through their superficial Catholicism. While this thin veneer of Catholicism was not made to last, it's also very difficult to remove it from the world, so I don't even try.

It's trendy to bash Christianity in my circles, but I think of it as an historical necessity/reality so I don't join in. I don't have any religious beliefs aside from encouraging participation in & understanding the history of traditions & I think Christianity has a lot to offer the world, but I think that belief gets in the way of engagement with reality. As a sidenote, it is important to understand that Catholicism is Christianity as pushed by the Roman Empire & Christianity is the religion that follows Jesus Christ in general. In Catholicism, Halloween began as Allhallowtide. Allhallowtide is a triduum (Three day holiday) of All Saint's Eve, All Saint's Day (also known as Hallowmas) & All Soul's Day & is a time to remember the dead which includes dead Saints & Martyrs. Allhallowtide means All Holy Time, showing that even the Catholics acknowledged that this period of time was different.

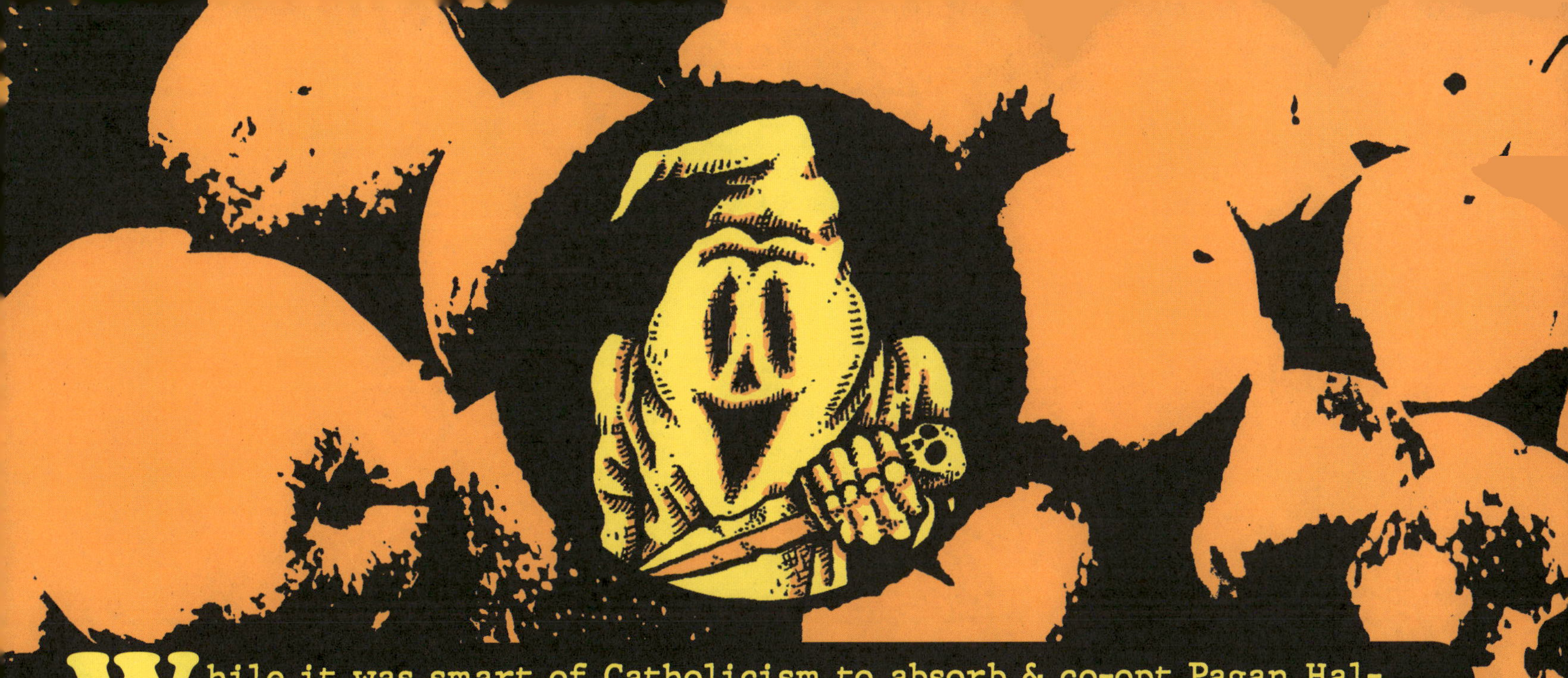

While it was smart of Catholicism to absorb & co-opt Pagan Halloween traditions instead of trying to destroy them, the innately non-Christian nature of the Holiday cannot be denied. Luckily the death-cult element of Catholicism (probably Pagan too) works well with the morbid theme of the holiday. Catholicism basically slapped a veneration for Saints, Martyrs & the faithful onto this time of death & weirdness in the air. Catholicism has more than ten thousand Saints, so the daily veneration of Saints only allows for 365, while All Saint's Day covers all the Saints. All Hallow's Eve is a vigil with candles & fasting time before the big feast on All Saint's Day. Then All-Souls Day follows where you honor the faithful that have died. Old English tradition had a predecessor to Trick or Treating called Souling. Souling was a kind of acceptable begging where Soulers would go from house to house performing songs & begging for beer, apples & Soul Cakes which were made specially for the holiday. Soul Cakes are hand-sized baked goods that are spiced & there is a cross carved into the top. Sometimes the Soul Cakes would be blessed in exchange for prayers for the dead. Kids going Souling would dress in costumes (possibly as Saints, but also as witches, skeletons, devils & ghosts) & carry turnip-lanterns.

Jack O' Lanterns got their start in Ireland where the people carved turnips into grotesque faces as part of Allhallowtide but also as part of Samhain. Pumpkins are a New World fruit & don't come into play until Europeans start exploring the Americas. Mythologizers want there to be a story & meaning behind the carved turnip lanterns but I imagine that people just wanted a light for carrying in such a dark time of year & turnips were relatively easy to carve & plentiful. People like to carve things & need light. The lore states that people believed that the lanterns held the soul of "Stingy Jack", a sly character that was lost wandering the Earth between Heaven & Hell until his body fell apart. Eventually Pumpkins replaced turnips & got locked in.

New Halloween Traditions

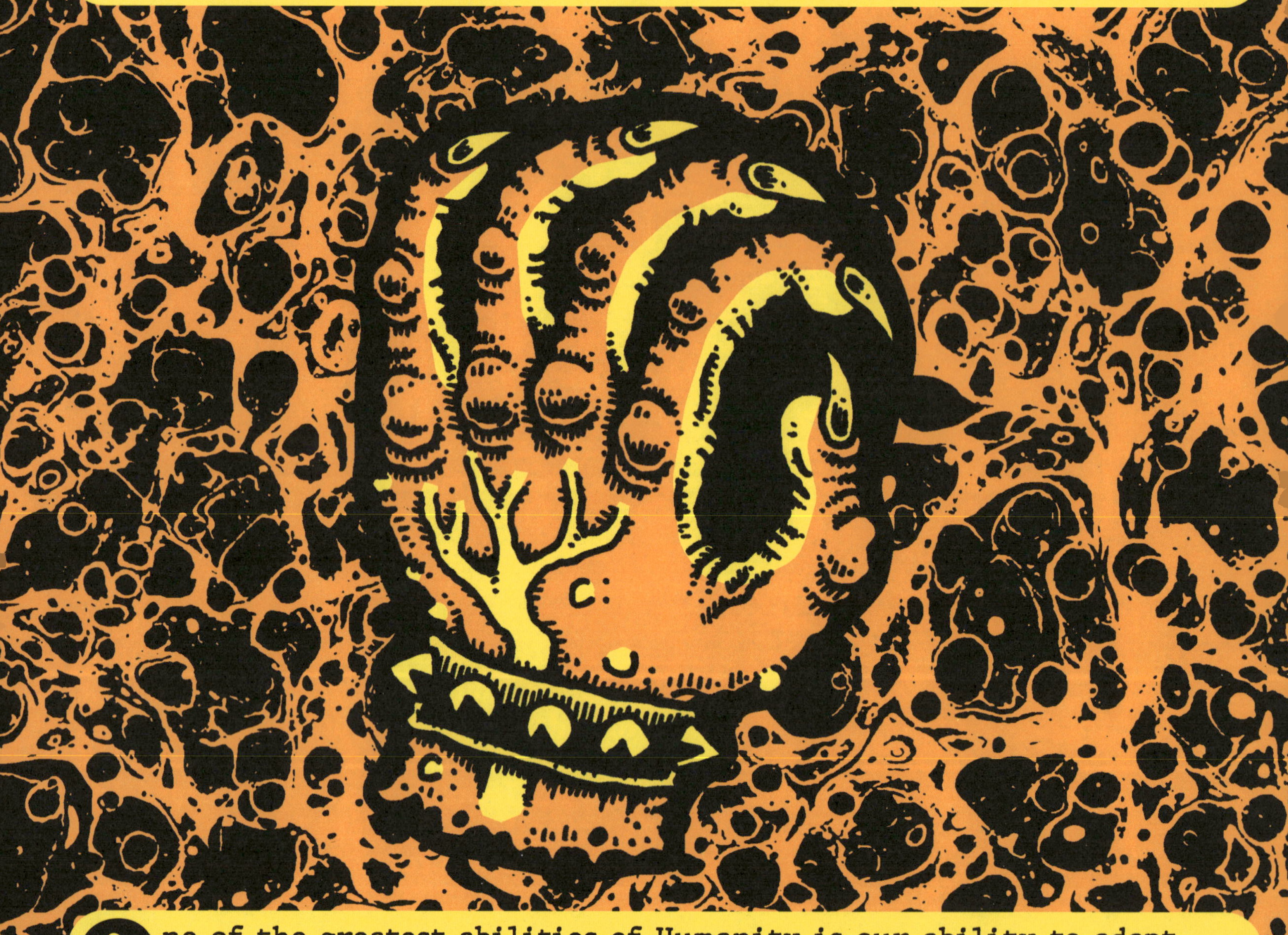

One of the greatest abilities of Humanity is our ability to adapt. Things keep on changing & we keep adapting! That said, not all adaptations are good because what we're adapting to is frequently not ideal or manufactured as something to react against by bad actors or our adaptation is ill advised. It is better to view our ability to adapt as a positive, because survival is the number one priority, but we must be flexible & reflective in the way we look at our adaptations & see them for what they are. Because of this we've got to look at the way we interact with culture & each other in a way that we never have. This has been a big part of my life work with GOBLINKO & is something I am still trying my hardest to communicate with people clearly. The best way I can communicate this idea is you must be forceful but also flexible, this is some cultural Kung Fu. All that said, Halloween has adapted & changed along with the times, for better or for worse.

As Halloween has become this holiday of becoming what you are not, lots of small bands dress up as bigger, known bands & cover their songs. This doesn't have a proper name but it is a tradition in almost every city in America that has a music scene. The most proper is bands covering a Halloween appropriate band (Alice Cooper, the Cramps, Misfits etc) but we know that people use Halloween as an excuse to dress up as anything. We ran a Rock&Roll magazine for almost ten years & only a handful of the bands we covered went anywhere & none of them got "big". This is just the reality of the music world, so these Halloween shows are a fun way to stir things up.

There is the kid's world of Halloween & there is the adult world of Halloween. Ultimately the ages shouldn't be separate, but our society is broken. In the adult world of Halloween, adults have lots of Halloween parties & it's largely an excuse for partying. One of the things that has come out of this age segregation is the advent of the "Sexy Everything" costumes for women. This used to be normal fantasies like the French Maid but has multiplied & devolved over time into things like "Sexy Pizza" or "Sexy Elmo". I'm sorry for polluting this book with these things.

The internet is fun because you can basically type in anything you can think of & you can buy it. This freedom is amazing but it also corrosive. In this freedom the variety of costumes is insane, you can dress as a dinosaur, a banana, anything you can imagine. But, this freedom has little to do with Halloween & has just furtherly confused people.

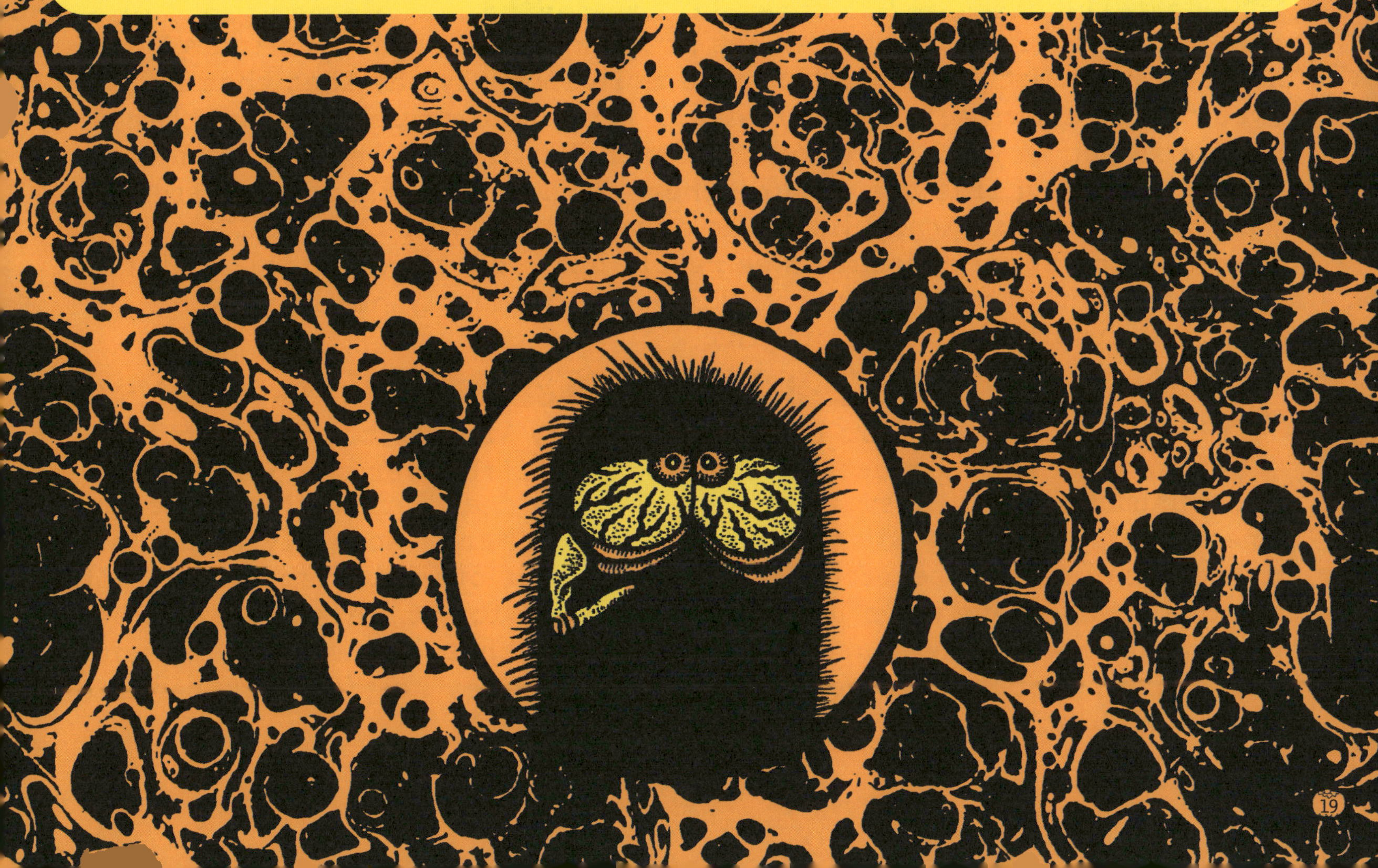

Part of the greatness of America is our freedom. This freedom comes at numerous costs, one of the costs is clarity & singularity. This freedom also emphasizes the parts of our lives where we are not free. One of the things we are not free from is this freedom of choice, so people become ludicrously rigid as a way of staving off the chaotic nature of their world. I don't have an answer to this issue, besides being conscious of it & trying to spread this consciousness to others.

The overtly Pagan roots of Halloween have lead to Christian Fundamentalists trying their damnedest to introduce things like Harvest Festivals & the like in place of Halloween celebrations. There is not anything wrong with these in general, it is harvest time afterall, but shutting out the majesty of Halloween is just doing people a disservice.

Trick or Treating just rubs certain kinds of people (control-freaks) the wrong way. Encouraging kids to dress up & run around in their neighborhood demanding candy under the threat of pranks sounds like fun to some, but insanity to others. In attempt to rein in this chaos, concerned citizens have introduced things like "Trunk or Treating" where kids get treats from cars or "Malloween" where kids go Trick or Treating at the mall. Civic minded adults should view Trick or Treating as an aspect of the health of their neighborhood.

As moralism & etiquette policing have passed from the right to the left, the chaos of Halloween is threatening a whole new group of pearl-clutchers for a whole new set of reasons. This started with a whole "My Culture Is Not A Costume" trend & more recently the idea that Halloween is somehow racially exclusive. I agree that dressing as another culture is not in good taste for Halloween, but mainly because Halloween is about dressing like the dead & other weird, morbid things, not stereotypes of Native Americans, Mexicans or what have you. I think it is better to understand these complaints as people obsessed with control aiming at something that is out of control. Halloween obviously has nothing to do with race, despite its Irish origins.

The rage to find racism everwhere is very similar to those people that were seeing traces of the Illuminati all over the place except with accusations of racism it is more of a big deal. I find this to be an unnecessarily divisive politic & question whether it actually benefits anybody it claims to benefit. There is plenty of overt racism to deal with that one doesn't have to go looking under rocks for it. This cause has been quickly co-opted by megacorporations in a way that has never been seen before. Again, you can side-step this whole issue by keeping a proper Halloween: Celebrating death & weird morbidity!

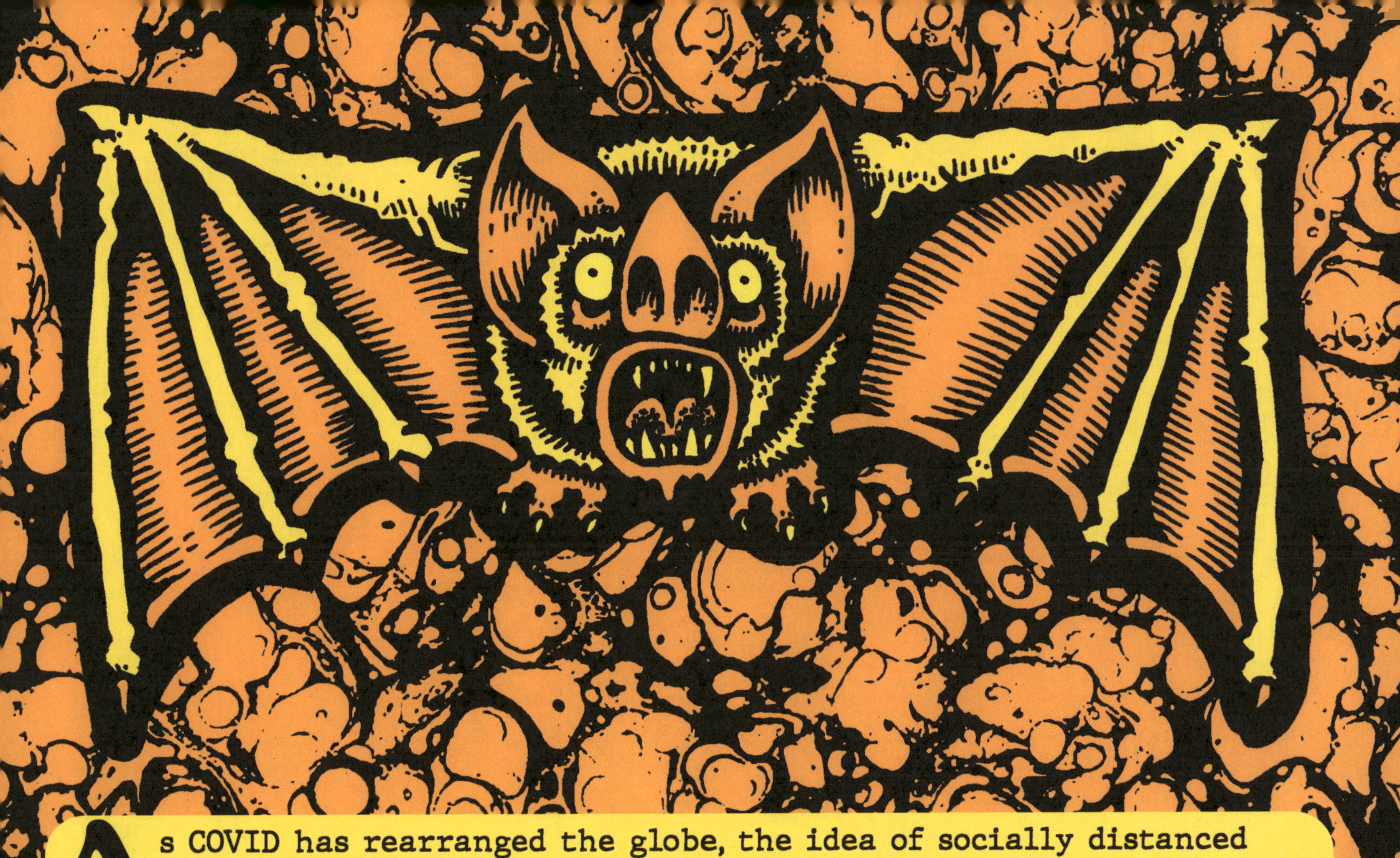

s COVID has rearranged the globe, the idea of socially distanced Trick or Treating has come up. People created elaborate methods of delivering treats without delivering COVID. Luckily Trick or Treaters already tend to wear masks, but going door to door in a pandemic does raise some issues. It was recommended that people go Trick or Treating outside & in small groups, both of which are the norm. COVID is a moving target & it tends to get better & then get worse as people relax, so I'm not putting a lot in here about it other than acknowledging that it's a game changer that shouldn't be ignored.

The chaotic window of time we're in allows for a high rate of cultural turnover. Luckily, in this period Halloween is getting more popular, even if the tradition of Trick or Treating has been on the wane for a while. For better or worse there are less kids being born across the planet & America is just less kid-centric. As our own kids are aging out of Trick or Treating & the number of kids coming to our house continues to be a light trickle, we're having to find a different focal point for Halloween. With this we watch horror movies all month, visit the graveyard, we think about those that have passed, we decorate the house, we eat foods that evoke Halloween & read scary stories. Thinking about death gives your life purpose & clarity. We try to extend Holidays so there isn't just a singular temporal focal point. You just use the commonly celebrated day as the peak & then extend the climb towards the peak in either direction. This is both fun & functional, you can keep the celebration going for a while but you also don't have the pressure of doing it all on one day with people losing their minds & ruining the day!

Trick or Treating

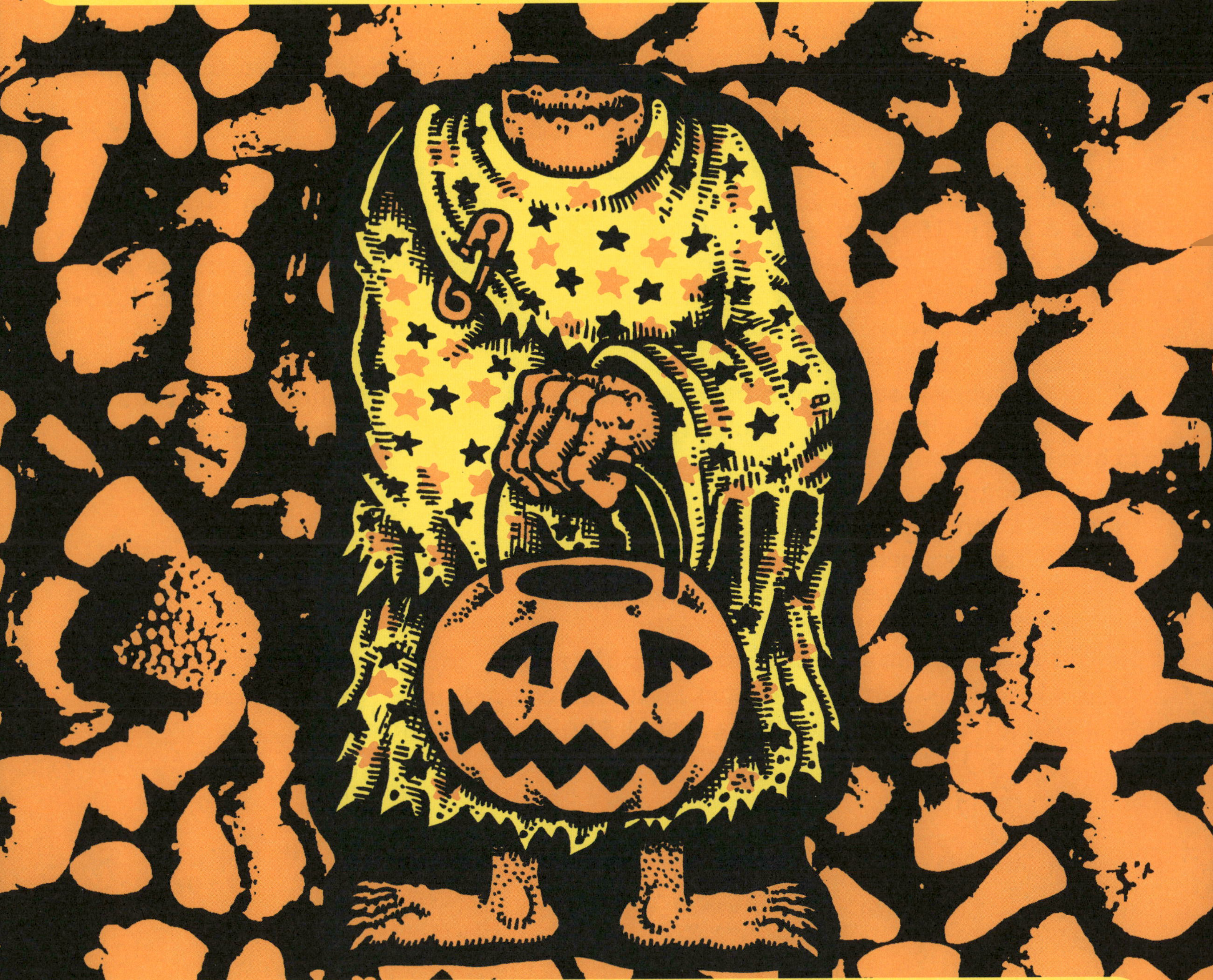

Trick or Treating is a glorious case of theatrical reenactment, but of what? Trick or Treating got its first mention in writing in 1927. While the trick element of Trick or Treating has been downplayed, you've got to acknowledge it or at least revere the tricks or else you'll get Devil's Night or Mischief Night where people commit arson! People need to blow off steam & misbehave, it just part of life!

People are always aging, that's just a fact of life, but birth rates are dropping too, so our Earth is becoming less child oriented, especially in the West. This has lots of effects but specifically we have less emphasis on Trick or Treating. With this fact, I feel like we are in the perfect moment to redo Trick or Treating for the future. We all know that America has been designed for cars & not people, most of us know that this is wrong. Part of the GOBLINKO vision of the future is to design cities for people not cars & with this people need to drop their paranoid vision of the world that helps to reinforce the idea that you need to roll around in a metal room to be safe. A lively Trick or Treating scene in your neighborhood partially indicates its health, because parents feel safe about letting their kids walk around at night taking candy from strangers. But we cannot wait for our cities to be redesigned & modified, we have to be ready for Trick or Treating NOW.

Change usually happens gradually, especially the kind of cultural change i'm advocating. So, Trick or Treating is going to be the way it is & dwindling unless we step forwards & show how it's done. Here is my plan for Trick or Treating. Don't get caught! Remember, these tricks are for people that aren't giving out treats, especially for people that decorate for Halloween but aren't giving out treats.

- Dress spooky, save your other costume ideas for another occassion.
- Make the threats of tricks real, but do minor tricks that aren't horrible.
  - Soap windows
  - Turn porch furniture upside down
  - Egg houses
  - Toilet paper houses & yards
  - Unscrew lightbulbs
- Trick or Treat in your own neighborhood, don't commute!
- A lit Jack O Lantern means that Trick or Treaters are welcome!
- Don't go Trick or Treating until the sun goes down.

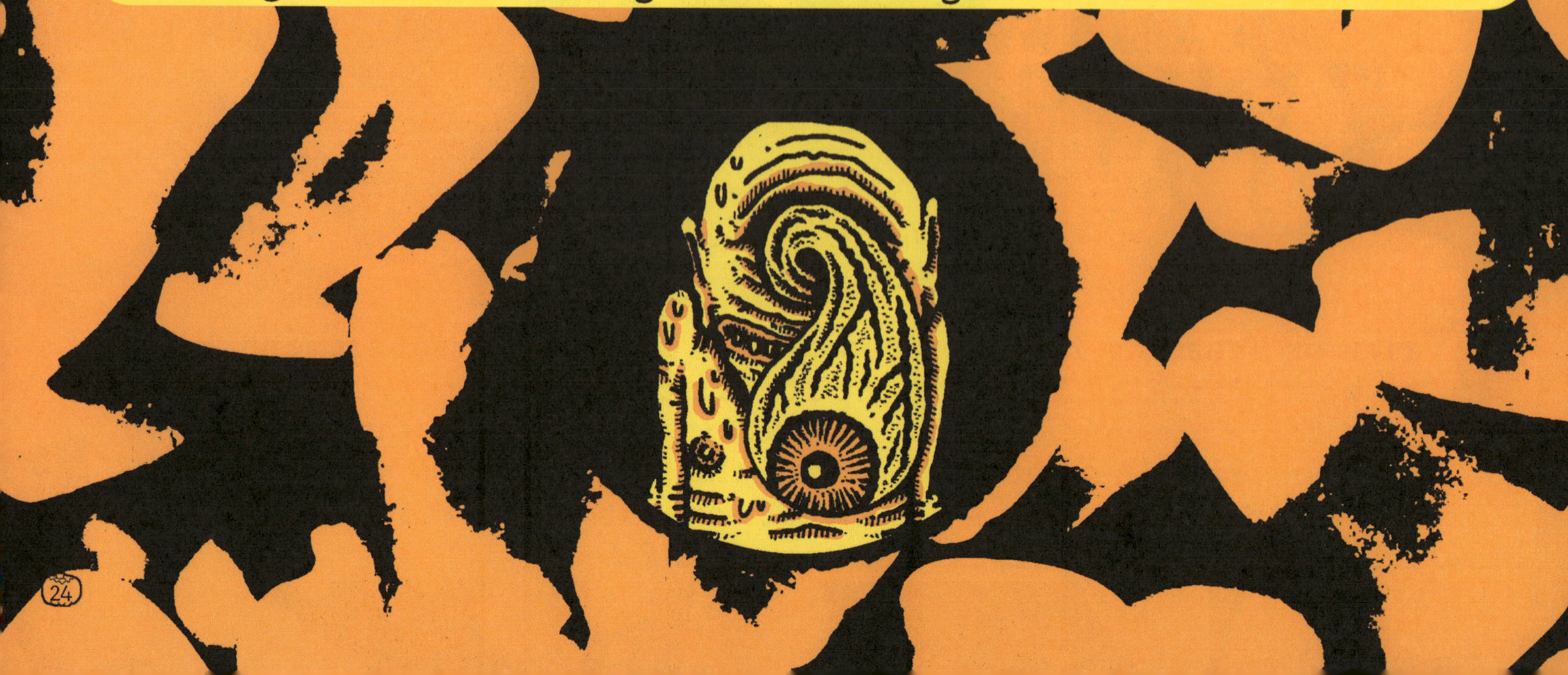

Ialways emphasize that Halloween is a morbid holiday. This is just one of my rules, dress spooky for Halloween. Because of this, we've always had a costume box of black shrouds & various masks for our kids, if they are after a new look for Halloween they can get a new mask, if you don't like masks you can wear some deathly makeup. The goal is to look like a host of the dead & ghosts & monsters.

Iam overly conscious of saying that there is a correct way to do Halloween, but I think you agree with me, there IS a correct way to do Halloween. In doing this, I'm providing a list of suggested Halloween costumes. Reminder, use your clever, non-spooky costume ideas for some other event, you might have to champion costume parties in your city, but I really think it is important to keep these things distinct. I also recommend that you make your own mask, which is much more interesting than store-bought masks. A good Halloween costume can be a cool skull mask & a black shroud! That's it! You can sell people on your costume with will power!

- Ghost
- Zombie
- Vampire
- Werewolf
- Witch
- Grim Reaper
- Scarecrow
- Goblin
- Graverobber

There are tons of specific monsters that you can pull from & you can even get wild & do things like Japanese Yokai or folk spirits from across the world! You can have fun researching them! You can come up with your unique take on these costume ideas & put your imagination to use!

Halloween Costumes

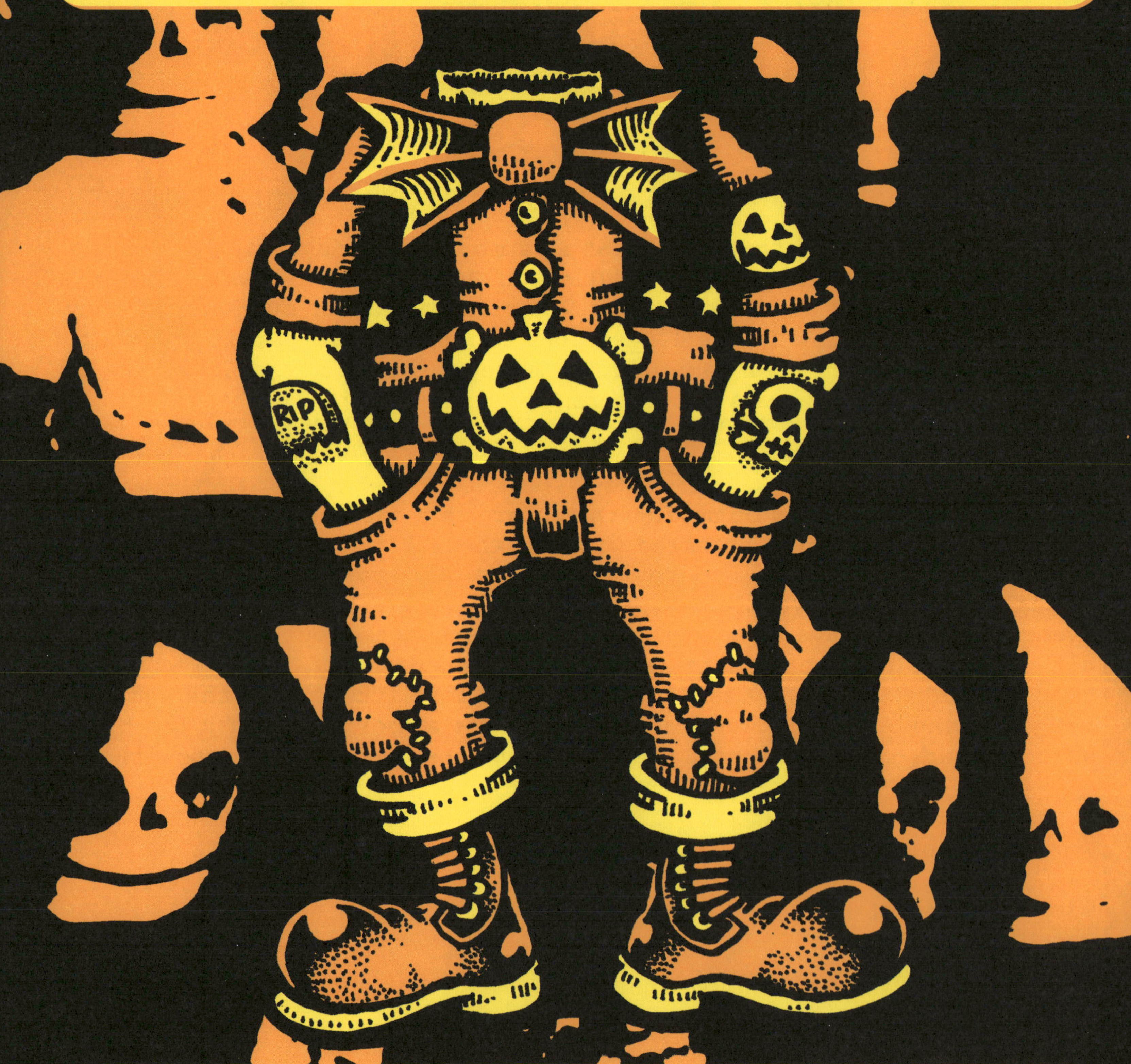

Halloween is about the world of the dead spilling into the world of the living. Dressing up for Halloween is a way of participating with this occurrence & get some treats in the bargain. Because of this, dressing up for Halloween has a ritualistic purpose & built-in aesthetic. Despite Halloween's liberatory elements, it's not about you, it's about death!

Every Halloween it becomes increasingly clear to me that people need better & more frequent excuses to dress up & be themself without judgment. Whether this is masquerade balls, going clubbing, various sorts of conventions, or what have you, Halloween shouldn't just be viewed as "the putting on a costume" holiday. Kids should have more days when they can dress up & be themself or not themself at school! Cowboys, princesses, superheroes, politicians, football players, cross-dressing & robots have nothing to do with Halloween, but have their own place as costumes certainly. Sure, you've got some clever ideas for costumes, but Halloween isn't about clever ideas. I'm trying to give Halloween some definition! As the door is closing for Halloween having an open costume element I want to introduce the potential for a lot of other doors opening to wear costumes. Even positing this rule, I get pushback because Halloween has filled the role of "Be Yourself" & "Dress Up" since World War II. I'm trying to separate these worthy elements from Halloween & reintroduce the dark core. My easy way of explaining this is that Christmas Trees are for Christmas & Valentines are for Valentine's Day. Halloween is about spookiness. If you went into a Spirit Store & were confronted by an animatronic princess you would be confused! Dressing up for Halloween has a purpose. If you don't understand this element of Halloween there is a reason you'd think that princesses have some part in this holiday. If your culture is transmitted to you by the people trying to sell you stuff, or by a broken society you're going to be confused! In trying to fix Halloween I am also trying to fix society. I acknowledge that this is a fool's errand, but it is a worthy one.

You have to use a treat when you're asking people to drop so much. I give more candy & compliments to kids that are dressing spooky. I don't speak negatively to the kids who aren't doing it right. If you think that more severe punishment is the way to go, hitting kids over the head with a baton for not dressing spooky would land you in jail & get your house targeted for arson. Ultimately, Halloween loses.

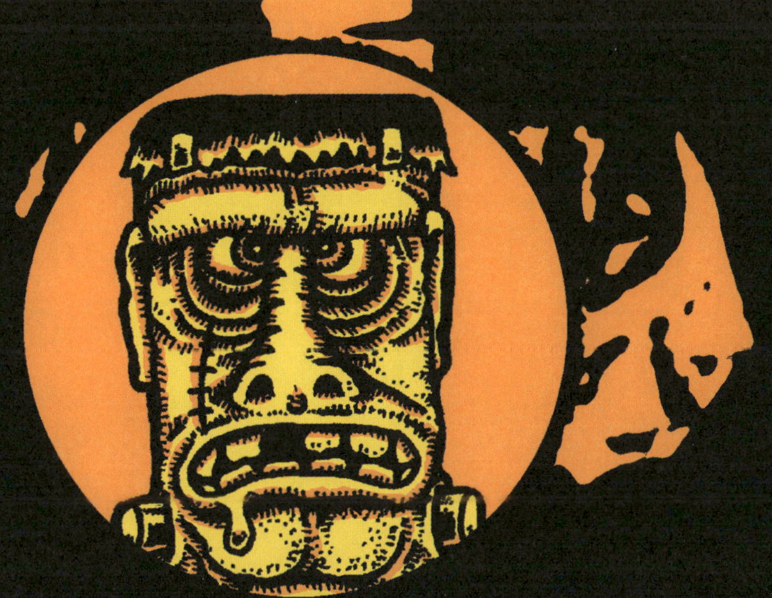

MY
NE
YE
NEX
YOUR
NAME
HERE
SEHN
2015
XIII

Jack o' Lanterns

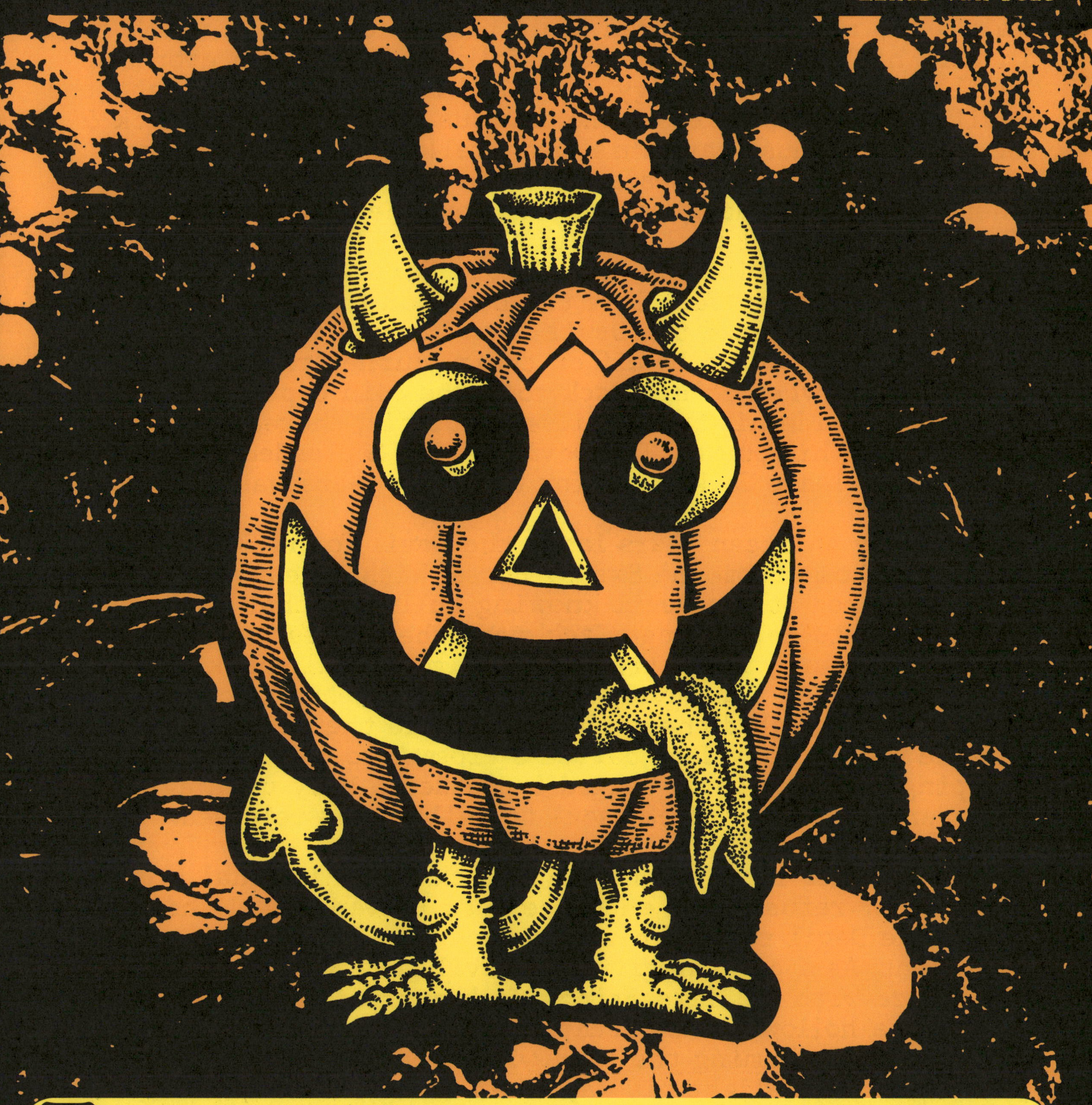

The Jack O' Lantern started as a turnip, hollowed-out & carved like a skull in Ireland & Scotland to ward off evil spirits, but with the advent of the American Halloween, the turnip was replaced by the Pumpkin. The pumpkin also lends its color, size & relatively hollow form to the task. This association with pumpkins dates back to at least the 1830s.

The Legend of Stingy Jack

Long ago in a small village in Ireland lived a terrible, stinky, dirty, mean, selfish, cowardly, tall, skinny drunkard named Stingy Jack. Jack was the kind of guy that kicked animals & was mean to children & old people for fun. He wasn't held in very high regard by the townsfolk, rightfully so, even the Devil was jealous of Stingy Jack's bad reputation. One night, the Devil overheard stories of the devious deeds of Stingy Jack & he decided he must have this nasty fellow's soul. Stingy Jack may have been a total bastard, but he was not feeble minded. When the Devil came to collect his soul, he made the case that the least the Devil could do was allow him to have a final drink at his favorite pub "The Sweaty Horse". The Devil agreed & after which, Stingy Jack left the Devil on the hook for the tab. Stingy Jack suggested the Devil turn himself into a coin to pay the bill & they would be off on their journey to Hell. The Devil was fooled when Stingy Jack took the coin & put it into his pocket alongside his trusty silver crucifix, thereby trapping the Devil in his pocket. The Devil begged & pleaded & only upon agreeing to leave Jack alone for thirteen years was he released.

Exactly thirteen years later, the Devil found Stingy Jack stumbling home from the Sweaty Horse. With a heavy sigh, Stingy Jack looked at the Devil knowing full well that he intended to drag him to Hell. Stingy Jack made the request of the Devil to climb a nearby apple tree to get him a final snack to eat before the journey. The Devil, apparently still not as clever as Stingy Jack, climbed the apple tree. While the Devil was climbing the tree, Stingy Jack carved a cross into the trunk, thereby trapping him. The Devil begged & pleaded & only upon agreeing to never take Stingy Jack's soul to Hell was he released.

Many years later, when Stingy Jack took his final breath, Saint Peter refused him entrance into Heaven for all his evil deeds. The Devil refused him entrance into Hell due to their agreement. As a parting gift, the Devil gave Stingy Jack an ember ablaze with hellfire. Stingy Jack carried this infernal flame in a hollowed out turnip. Stingy Jack was stuck as the walking dead, roaming the land with a carved turnip glowing with hellfire to light his way. When Stingy Jack's rotting body finally ceased to be, Jack of the Lantern began. On Halloween night, keep an eye out for a restless wandering soul every time you see a Jack O' Lantern, for it may just be the glowing hellfire from Stingy Jack's lantern.

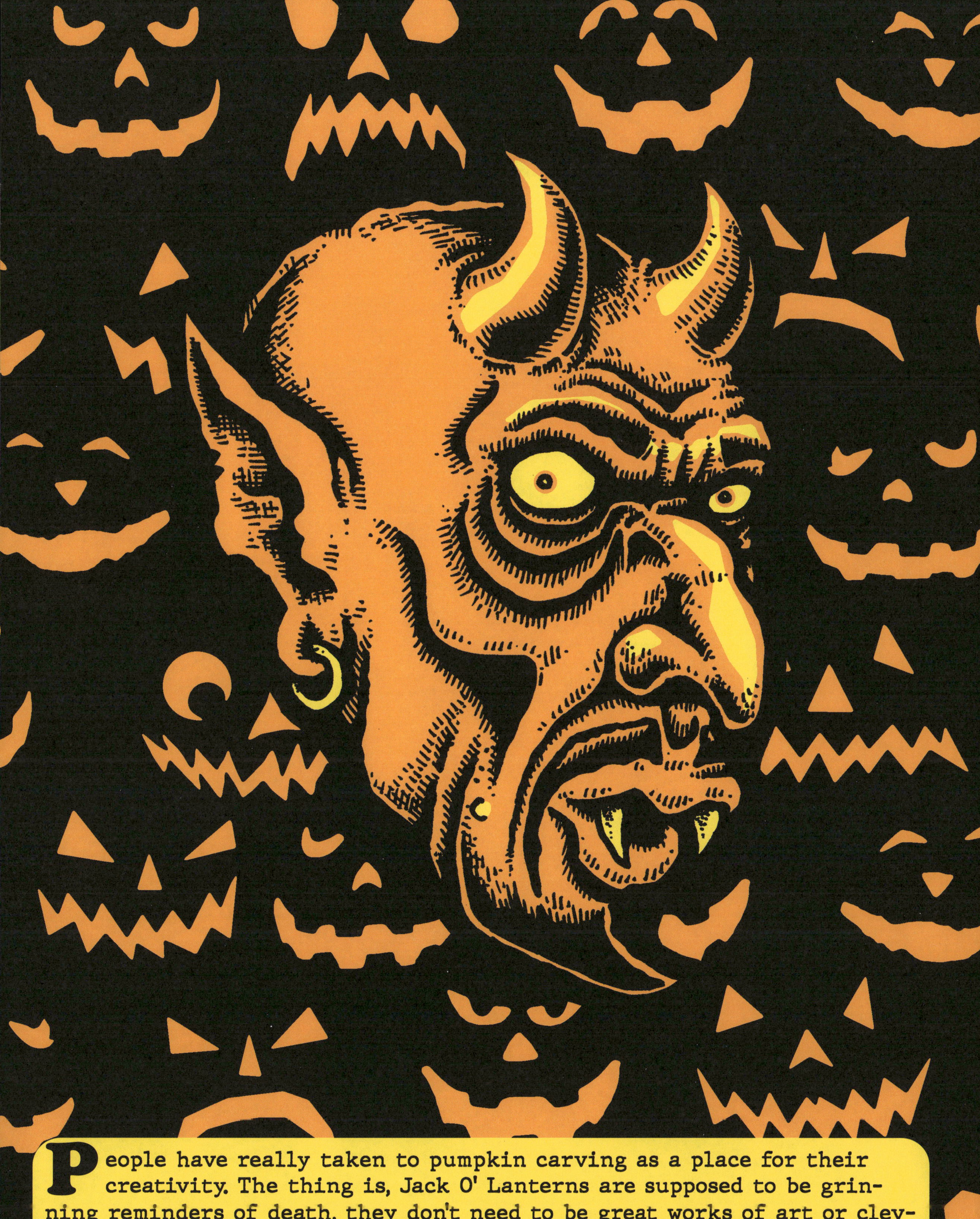

People have really taken to pumpkin carving as a place for their creativity. The thing is, Jack O' Lanterns are supposed to be grinning reminders of death, they don't need to be great works of art or clever jokes. My take is that if you want to elaborately carve food, watermelons, butter & ice are calling your name.

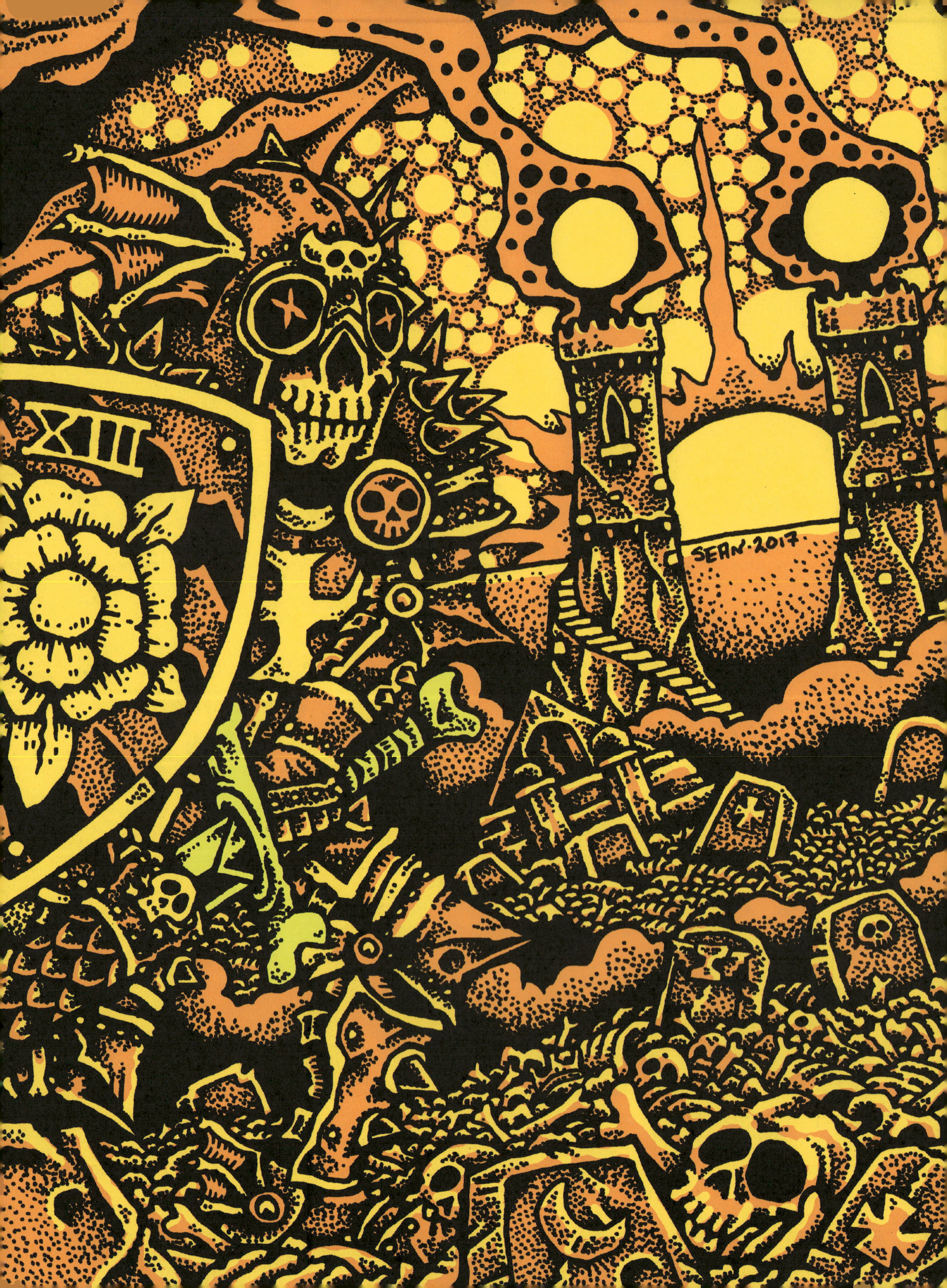

XIII
SEAN·2017·

Death

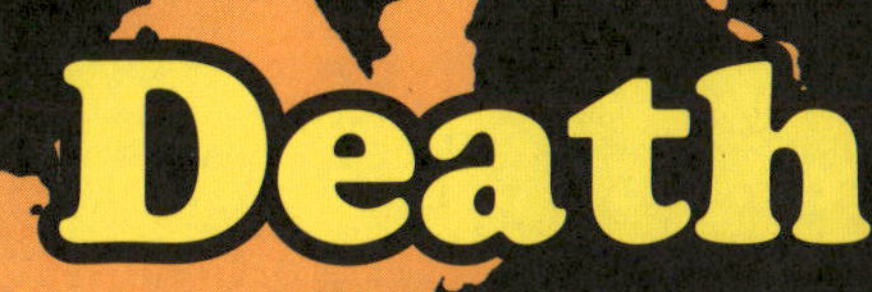

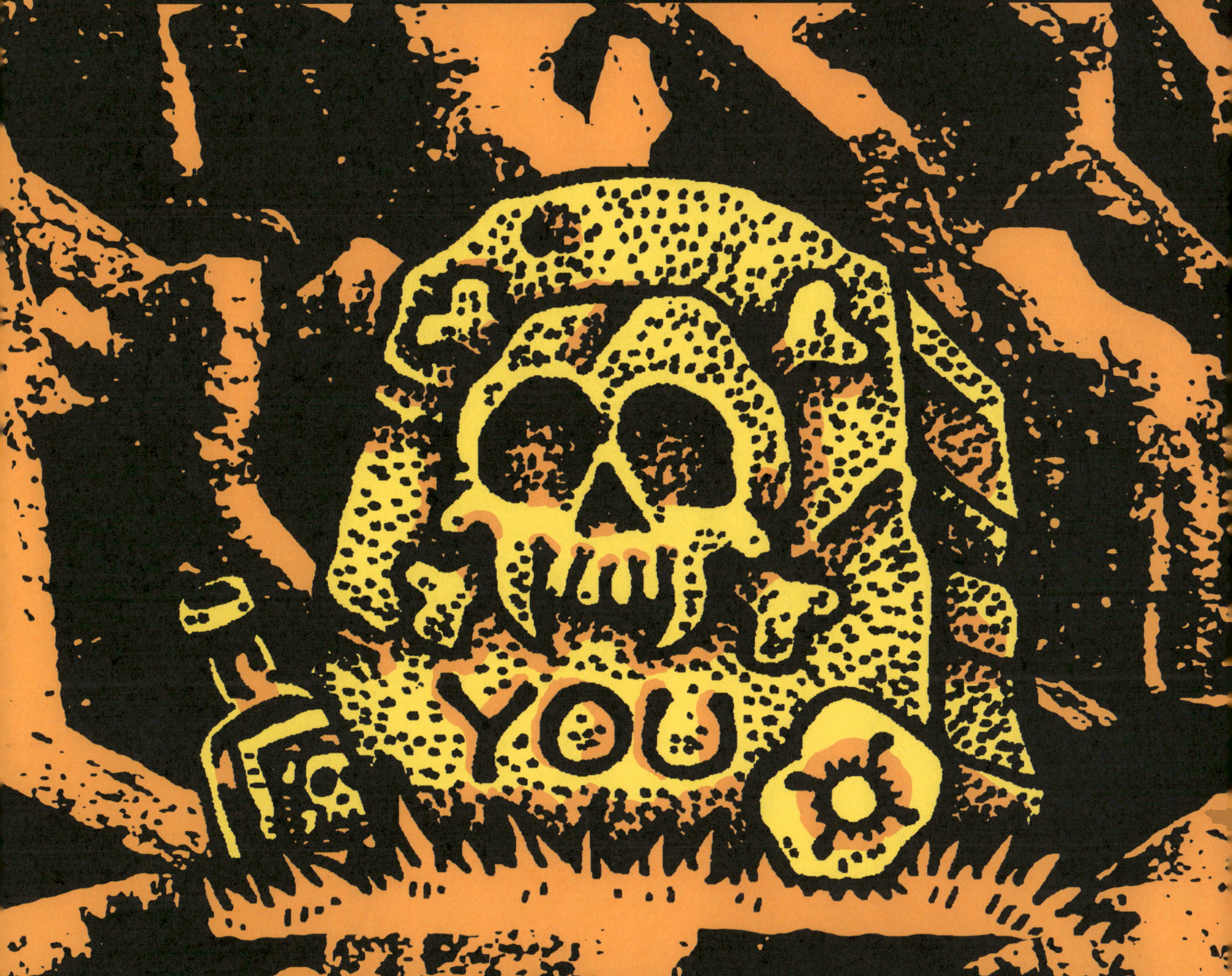

Halloween is all about death. But it's not an alienated fear of death, in some ways it is a celebration of death embodied by the grinning skulls that are Jack O' Lanterns. Legend has it that the veil between worlds is thinnest on Halloween, allowing spirits to travel freely during this time. Halloween should incorporate some aspect of reverence for the dead in it or else you're not understanding the holiday. Everyone dies, but most people aren't prepared to face death. Halloween can & should be a little yearly meditation on death. This isn't to suggest that death isn't sad or a loss, but it's a constant that should be acknowledged for the sake of everybody & their general psychological well-being.

Everyone dies, there's just no way around it. When humanity was more at the mercy of nature, people saw more death around them, their lives were shorter, there was more infant mortality, they had to kill to eat, there was just more connection to death in general. This isn't positive or negative, but how we live now is different & particularly divergent from how we evolved. Our egos are terrified of dying, because that is the nature of the ego. Halloween can & should be a time to think about death, it doesn't have to be heavy, it is sweetened by treats! You get used to thinking about death, more comfortable with it the more you engage with it. So, I think about death a lot during Halloween & the surrounding times. I think about people close to me that have died, recently, in the past, even before I was born! I also think about people that will die, but haven't yet. I think about how I died & came back & how things would be if I hadn't! Most people are uncomfortable with thinking about death in this way, but it's reality, we all die, everything dies, it's unavoidable. Meditating on death makes you live better. Plants die in the winter, farm animals die so that we can eat, the sun goes down every day. Everything has a beginning & an end. It's not tragic, it's reality. GOBLINKO had a series of buttons for Rock&Rollers who "Gave Their Life". This was not to emphasize their death, but to recognize that they had given their life to something bigger than them. Even if they didn't give their lives in service, or personally recognize that they had, they gave their lives as a symbol that others could recognize, consciously or not! As humanity trundles along, the deaths outnumber those alive! We need to think & live as if we were already dead!

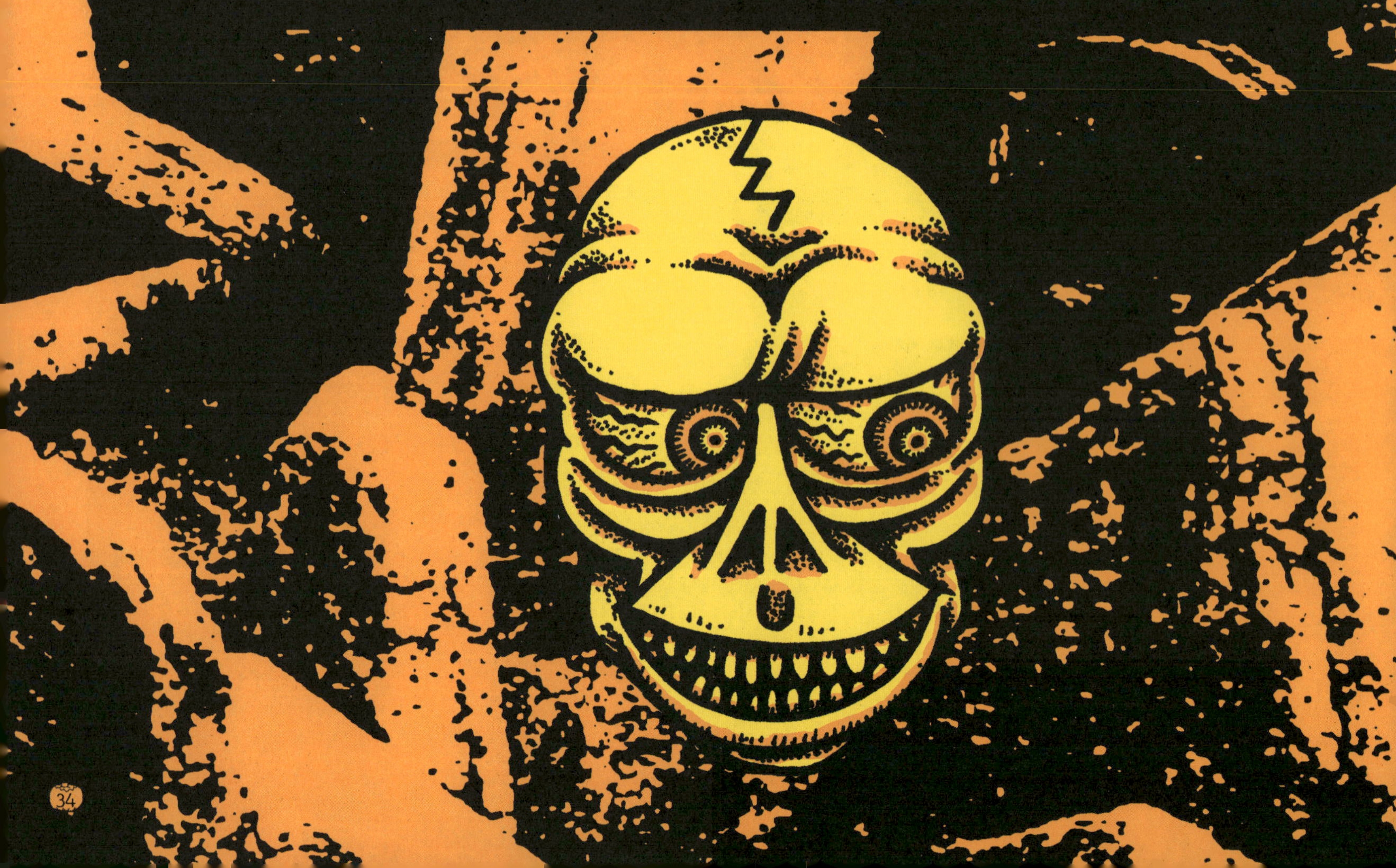

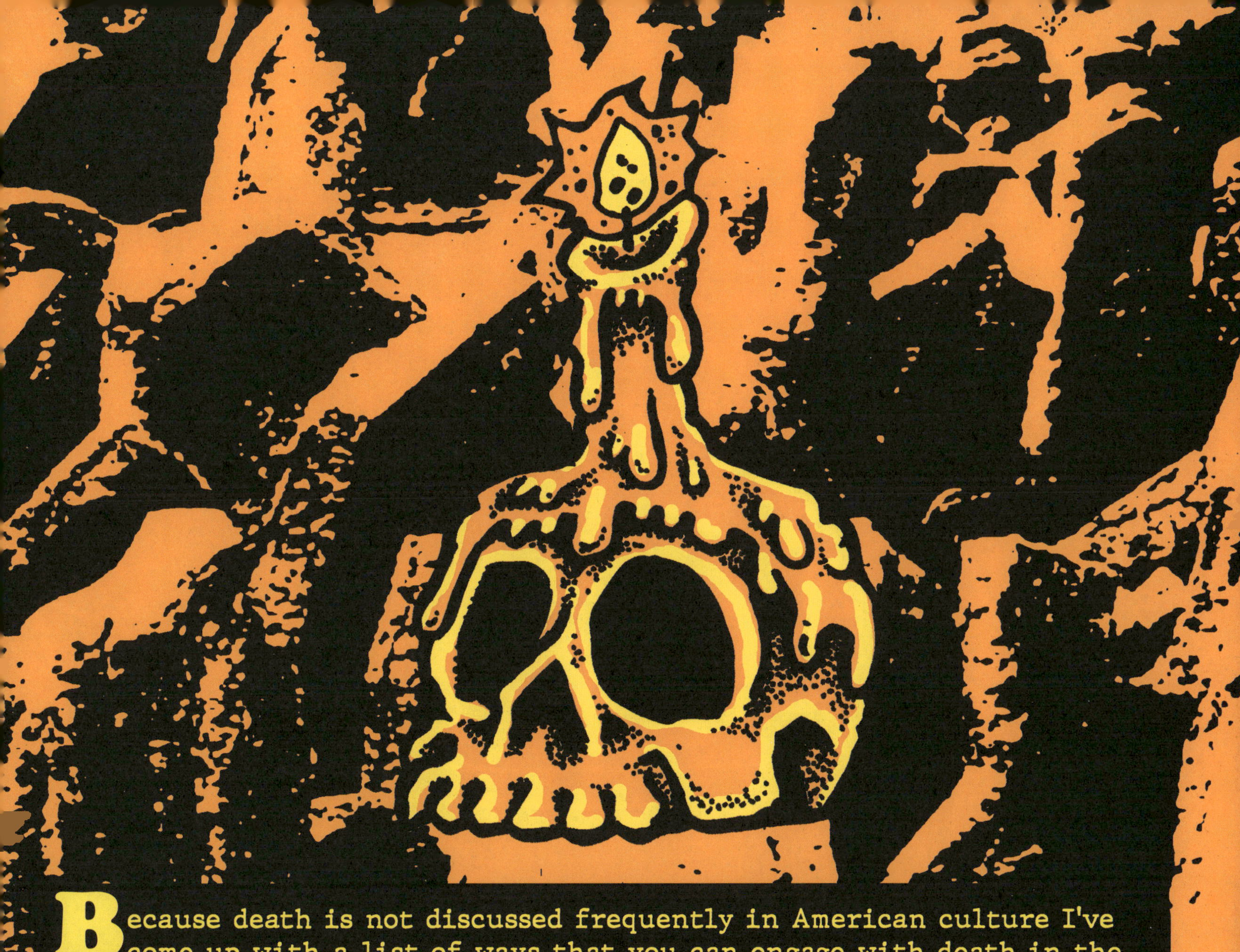

Because death is not discussed frequently in American culture I've come up with a list of ways that you can engage with death in the Halloween time. Again, the point in this is not negative or depressive, remiunders of death should make you live better!

☻ Decorate with skulls & bones during Halloween, it works with the holiday & reminds you of what lies beneath your skin & flesh.

☻ Put up photos of loved ones that have died.

☻ Imagine that you're going to die next year, are you living how you should be? Are you doing things as if you were going to be gone soon?

☻ Carve your Jack O' Lanterns into skulls & think about death.

☻ Use a Ouija Board to contact the dead, or conduct a seance.

☻ Wear or carry a Momento Mori with you, or even get it tattoo'd on you.

☻ Visit a graveyard & think about all those people that lived & died & ended up at that resting spot.

Halloween Eats

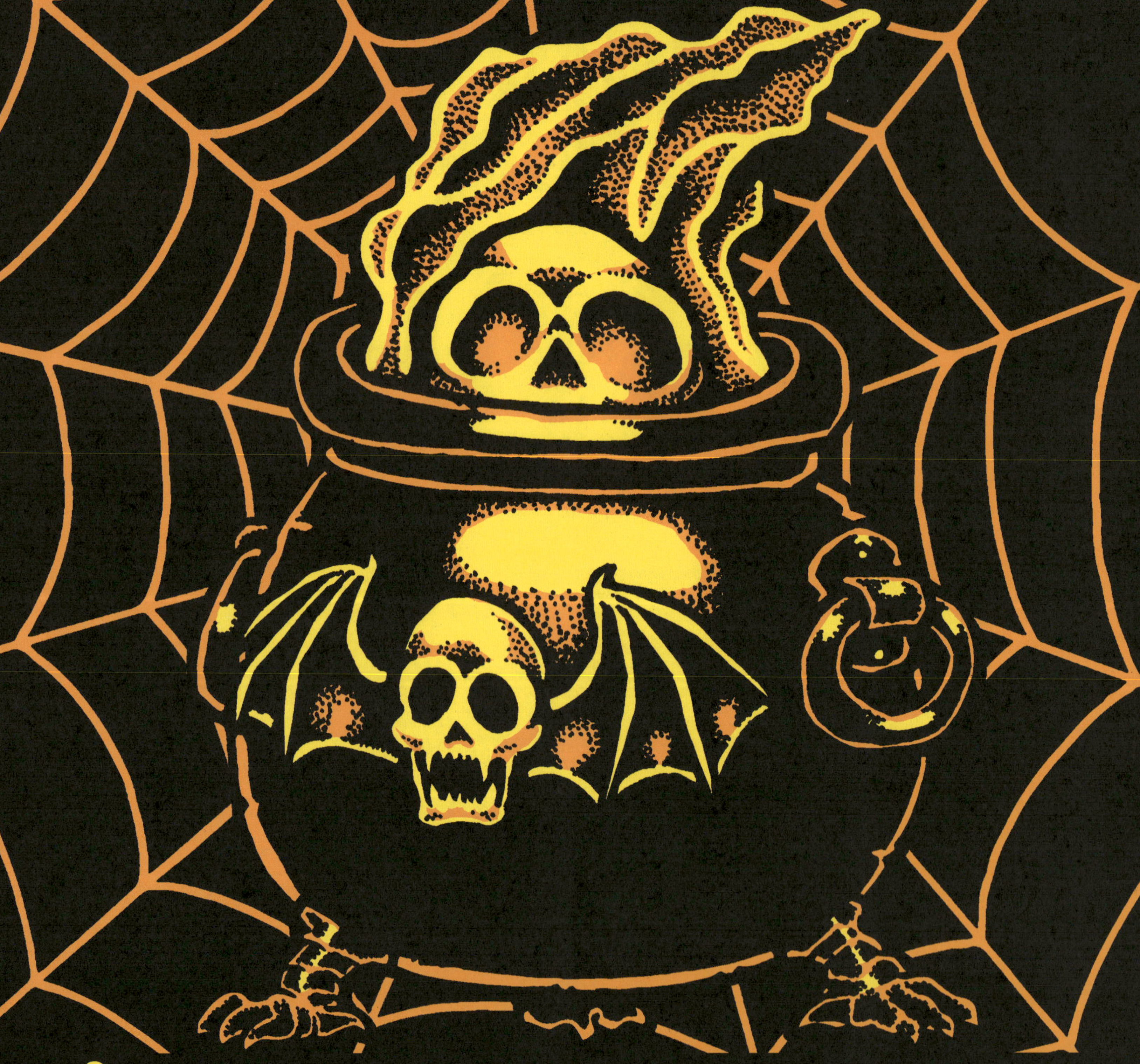

All holidays have a feast associated with them. Halloween has the traditional candy haul & gluttonous consumption thereof, but I feel like people would do better with more & healthier options! With that in mind, i'd like to share some Halloween eating ideas. I'm not including recipes in this section because these are just suggestions & inspirations & you can look up recipes yourself in your favorite locations.

Halloween has become so defined by Trick or Treating that there aren't any foods associated with the holiday that aren't sweet treats. Observant Italian Catholics eat certain traditional foods on All Saints Day but these haven't made their way to the new world in any noticable way. The pumpkins of Halloween should be extended into the cuisine of the time & for some reason I associate chili & hot dogs with Halloween, so let's go with that also, I present you with 13 meal plans for your Halloween celebration!

1.

🎃 Corn Dogs (you could emphasize the corn in the batter by adding whole corn kernels or just adding more corn meal).
🎃 Cole Slaw with Apples
🎃 Tortilla Chips

2.

🎃 Chili (use a variety of beans & a can of corn)
🎃 Corn Bread with Whole Corn Kernels
🎃 Garnish the Chili with chopped onions, grated cheese & jalapenos.

3.

🎃 Pumpkin Curry (This one can be done Vegan really easily)
🎃 Rice (use brown rice to increase the healthiness)
🎃 Thai Salad Rolls

4.

🎃 Meatloaf (fashion it into a morbid shape like a human corpse.)
🎃 Mashed Potatoes (leave the skins on)
🎃 Roasted Brussels Sprouts (this has rehabilitated this vegetable)

5.

- Chili Dogs using leftovers from the chili you made previous
- Sauerkraut (use Kimchi if you wanna go international)
- Frito Style scooping Corn Chips

6.

- Pumpkin Soup (many recipes for this, try a bunch)
- Fresh Bread that goes with your chosen soup

7.

- Sausage rounds, cauliflower & garlic with noodles (I like Rotini)
- Green Salad (Use lots of garlic to keep Vampires away)

8.

- Pumpkin Ravioli (try making them at home, they're easier than you think)
- Green salad (Go garlic crazy again)

9.

- Baked Beans (You can really easily make these Vegan or you can add Pork)
- Corn Bread with corn kernels
- Greens with Garlic (they might be crying for bacon)

10.

- 🎃 Corn Chowder (You can make it creamy or clear)
- 🎃 Fresh Bread (sourdough works great)
- 🎃 Green Salad with corn kernels

11.

- 🎃 Thai Corn Fritters with Sweet Chili Sauce
- 🎃 Green Papaya Salad
- 🎃 Fried pumpkin Slices

12.

- 🎃 Pancakes with Pumpkin Spiced Whipped Cream
- 🎃 Bacon (splash out & get the expensive stuff)
- 🎃 Breakfast Sausages
- 🎃 Apple Sauce (the sweetened kind is unnecessary)

13.

- 🎃 Grilled Sausages (use a variety of high quality ones)
- 🎃 German Potato Salad (served hot! Very different from American Potato Salad)
- 🎃 Red Cabbage Slaw

bonus

Halloween is a time of endless treats so I'm not including desserts but here are some ideas. Give them to Trick or Treaters to surprise people!

- 🎃 Donuts (make them at home!)
- 🎃 Caramel Apples
- 🎃 Gelatin Mold with Gummi Worms
- 🎃 Popcorn Balls

Pumpkin Spice

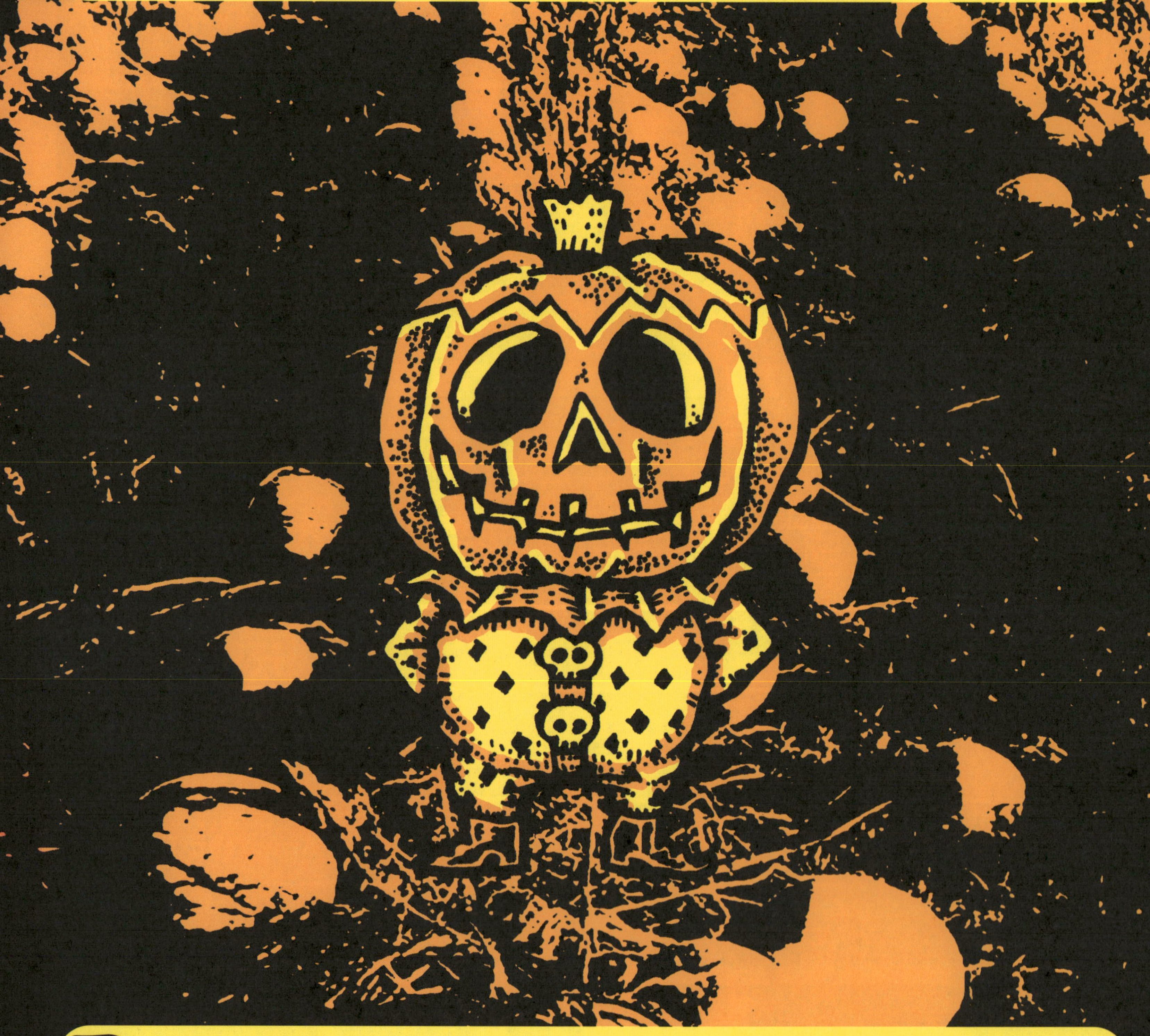

Pumpkin Spice, like Halloween has been captured by big business. Instead of having your life defined by & being a slave to big business Pumpkin Spice peddlers using you like a sack of potatoes, make your own! If you make your own, you can become notorious for your amazing, personal Pumpkin Spice blend. So, as with everything you do, I recommend you do it yourself & make it your own. But don't be afraid to enjoy the commercial options out there because there are a lot!

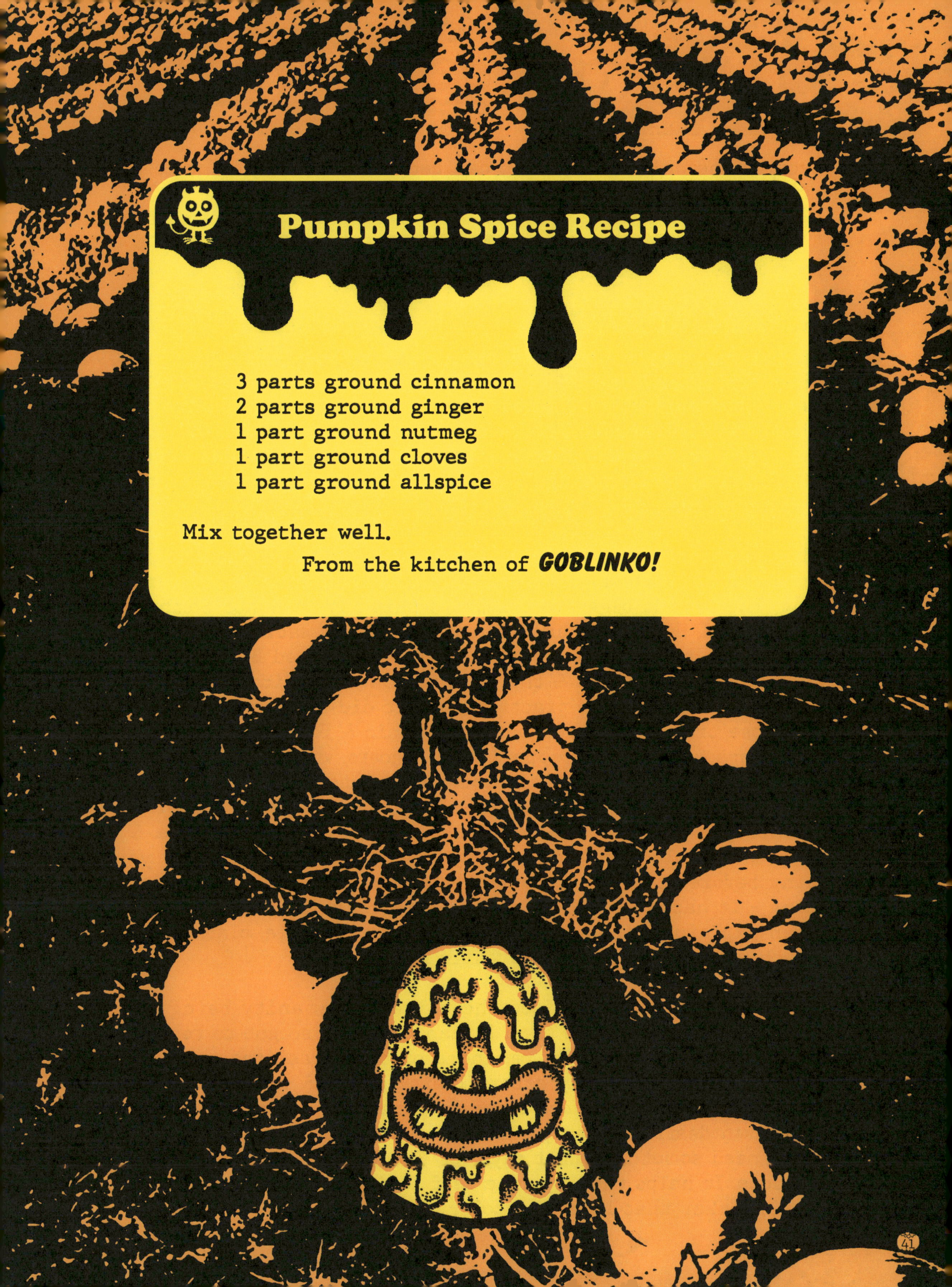

Pumpkin Spice Recipe
3 parts ground cinnamon
2 parts ground ginger
1 part ground nutmeg
1 part ground cloves
1 part ground allspice
Mix together well.
From the kitchen of GOBLINKO!
41

Halloween Icons

When I was very young, my favorite record was Oscar Brand's 1979 album "Trick or Treat." I think it's best to sum him up as a Folky historian, aspects of which I embody. This record both resonated with me & shaped me simultaneously. The record takes form as Oscar welcoming a bunch of Trick or Treaters into his house to proselytize the true meaning of Halloween through songs & stories. I quote the following from the record's liner notes.

"The Celts celebrated New Year's Day on November 1st. It was a logical choice, for the harvest was in & the cold white silence of winter was approaching. The Druids began to celebrate this day to honor Samhain, the Lord of the Dead. Honoring Samhain usually meant sacrificing horses & human beings in his name. When the Romans conquered Britain in 61 AD they outlawed the sacrifice & the celebration. This didn't prevent the Druids from continuing the practices, but it did cut down on the publicity. Since those primitive times, our folk music & folk lore have been overloaded by songs & ballads of apparitions, ghosts, witches, demons, goblins, & other unwelcome personalities. From the thousands of old songs, we have chosen an LP-full. We've enlightened these by a few erudite explanations. We have enlarged these by the use of supernatural sound effects. & we have given the whole a twisted ending worthy of the holiday. If you guess the ending before it arrives, score one for your paranoia. We didn't guess the ending - it happened suddenly & unexpectedly in the studio, & has never been explained. If any of this is understandable, blame Samhain… he wrote this collection of notes while I watched".

From that tender age I recognised the value of humanity being a vehicle for something, in being more than human. You've also got to teach people the right way to do things. I'm reminded of the Israelites worshipping Ba'al in the desert so quickly after fleeing Egypt & needing to be held on track. In my own life I have tried to personify some different things, even if my own desire to be myself has been at the heart of these embodiments. So I need something that says "Be Yourself", which Halloween ultimately does. It helps that my true self is a goofily morbid, anti status quo, trouble maker that loves the color orange & pumpkins!

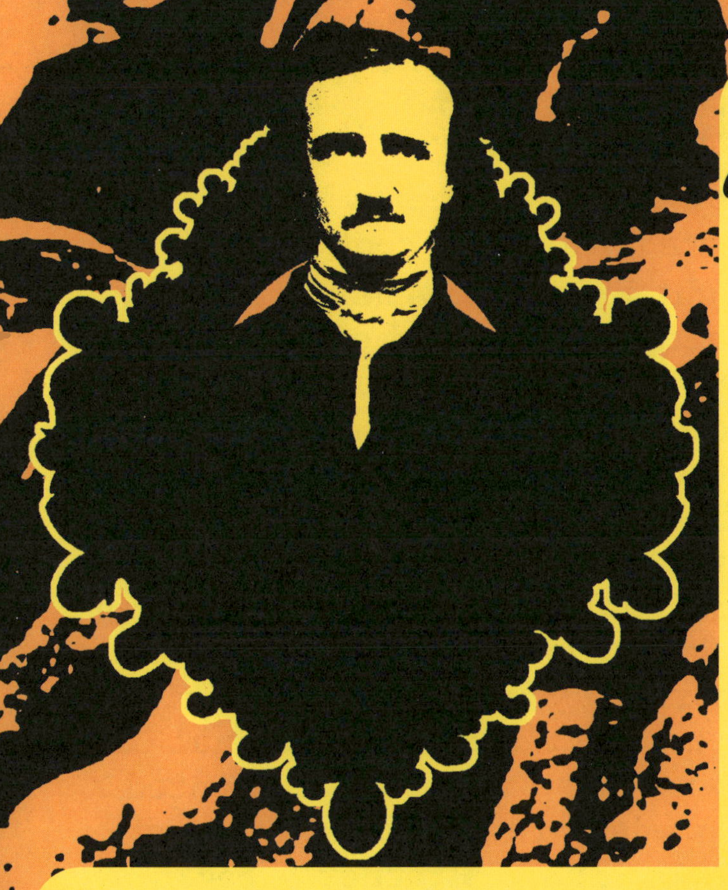

Edgar Allan Poe

The spooky literature godfather, Edgar Allan Poe was born in Boston, Massachusetts in 1809. He was possibly the first American writer to scrape a living from writing exclusively, because of this he left behind a lot of work & was even known during his life as a literary critic. Poe wrote poetry, short stories, a play & some journalism & he is best known & included here as an unmatched purveyor of Gothic Romanticism. His pieces "The Raven", "The Tell-tale Heart" & "The Pit & The Pendulum" have spawned countless interpretations (a lot of them starring Vincent Price). Poe helped invent the genres of Detective Fiction & Science Fiction. Like so many of the figures portrayed here, Poe is a guiding influence & their careers are inspired by him. Poe lived a short, tragic life worthy of one of his own stories & died outside a bar in Baltimore.

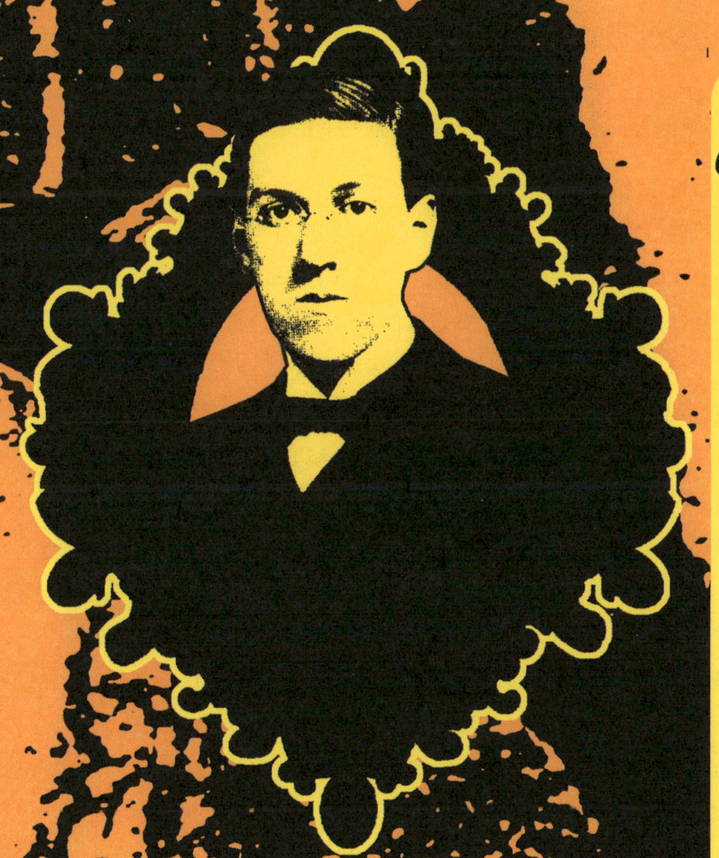

H.P. Lovecraft

The master of Cosmic Horror. Howard Philips Lovecraft peered past the veil & into the world of unseen horrors that dwell in other dimensions that view humanity as some insignificant dust. Lovecraft was born in Providence, Rhode Island in 1890. Lovecraft wrote Supernatural Horror fiction that would fit into the Science Fiction genre that was sweeping the globe. While horror has always used the fear of the unknown as its central theme, Lovecraft summoned up an entire new unknown to torment people with. This theme was so new to the genre that it was given Lovecraft's name as it's own. Lovecraft has gone from being relatively unknown in his lifetime, to a cult figure, to having some mainstream familiarity to revulsion at his personal beliefs, but it is important to remember that in Lovecraft's cosmology there is a big universe out there just waiting to make humanity irrelevant.

Vincent Price

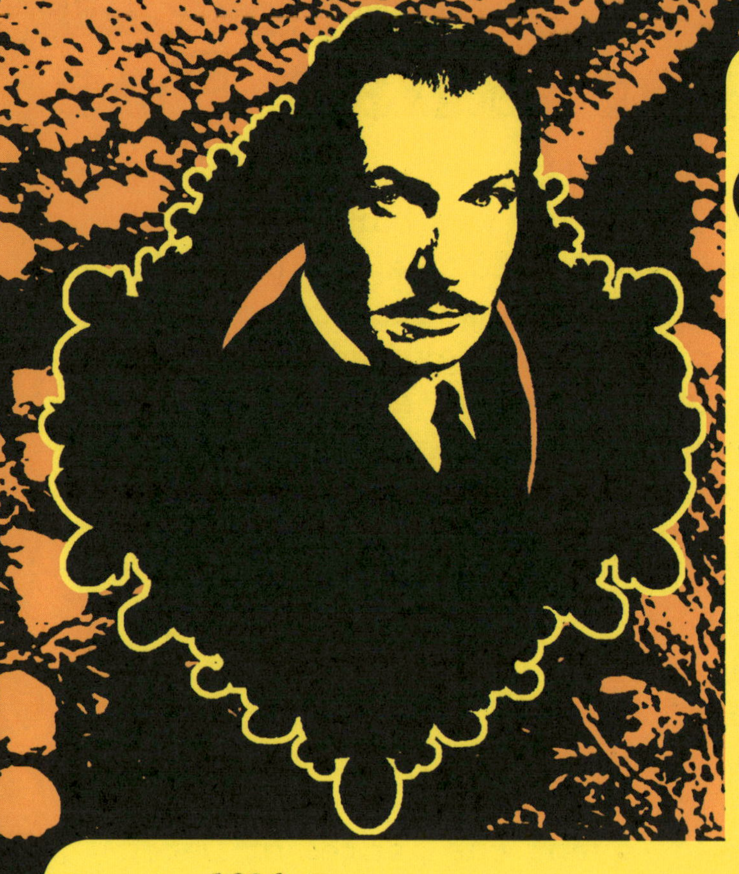

Campy, debonair, spooky & sophisticated. An actor, cook & art lover; Vincent Price was America's weird uncle that was the kind of character that you'd read about in a horror novel, not an ordinary, boring person by any stretch of the imagination. He was the kind of person that could say paragraphs with just the arch of an eyebrow. Price originally tried to be a leading man in Hollywood, but he got typecast (not incorrectly) as a campy villain. Born 1911, the heir of the National Candy Company (his father also invented a baking powder), in St. Louis. Price attended Yale like his father & began acting in 1936. Price went on to be in over one hundred movies, TV cameos, voice overs, commercials & the whole deal. It took Price until 1953 to get his first horror role under his belt & it just snowballed from there until he couldn't be separated from the genre.

Charles Addams

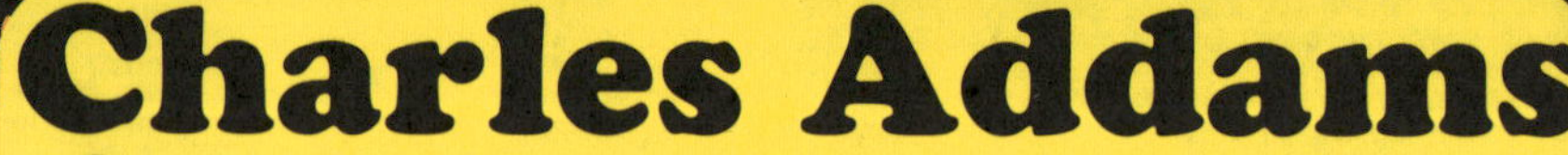

An unparallelled cartoonist of the macabre, Charles Addams was born in New Jersey in 1912. He rose to prominence drawing cartoons for the New Yorker but he also did work for other publications including TV Guide & Colliers. Eventually he came up with a set of cartoon characters that would come to be called "The Addams Family." The Addams Family would go on to be their own TV show, a cartoon & two separate movie series adaptations. The Addams Family featured a series of characters that made up a stark counterpoint to the straight-laced, post-war nuclear family. The Addams Family were a funhouse mirror held up to what America was trying to present itself as. They were a black clad, morbidly goofy, intergenerational, historically bound group of eccentrics that lived in a museum-like house & stood out from their starchy neighbors.

Alfred Hitchcock

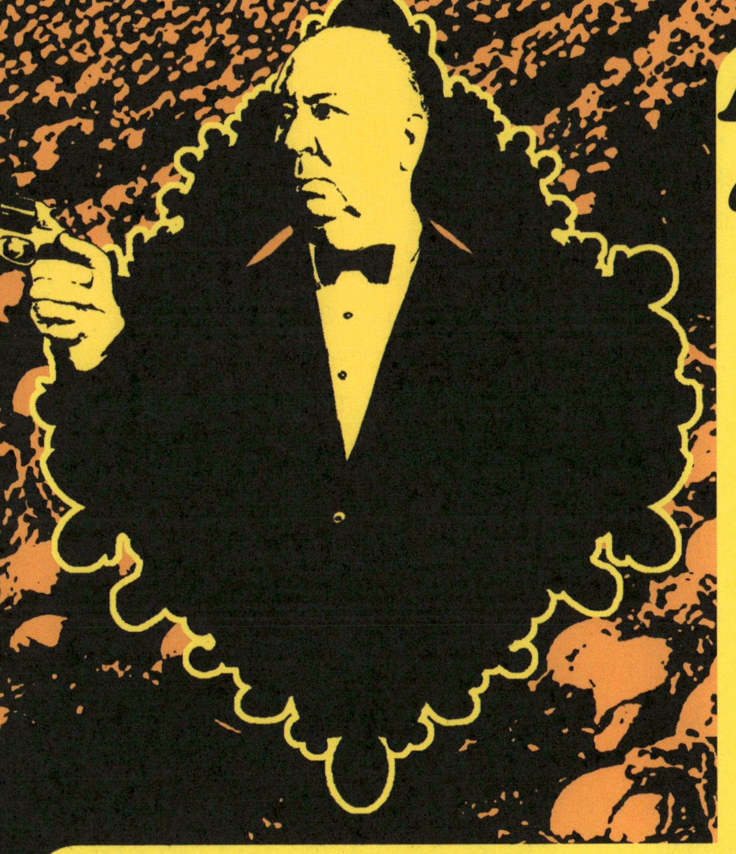

The Master of suspense, that is, what you don't see. Alfred Hitchcock was born in London, England in 1899. Hitchcock is one of the best & most revered movie makers of all time but also emphasized the macabre in all of his work. He made the first English "Talkie" in 1929 called "Blackmail". Over the decades Hitchcock made countless classics, most of which had a macabre angle. While Hitchcock's movies tended not to deal with traditional horror or supernatural themes common to the genre, he dwelled in & perpetuated a morbid cosmology of murder & intrigue that set the backdrop for a more realistic portrayal of the world that plays into the fun of Halloween. For the Hitchcockian world to play right, people must (correctly) suspect that awful things are waiting to happen, just off of camera.

Alice Cooper

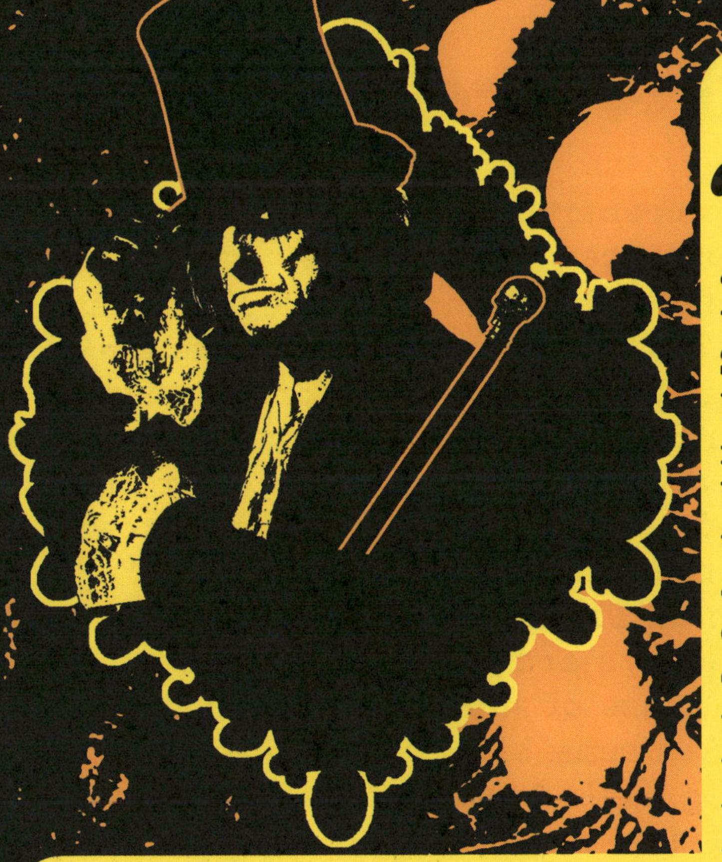

The Edgar Allan Poe of Rock&Roll. Rock&Roll used to be more associated with Halloween, when Rock&Roll was more of a threat to the status quo. So you gotta hold that ideal in your heart like I do. Funnily enough, Alice Cooper is the character of another Vincent, Vincent Furnier, born in Detroit, 1948. Vincent keeps Alice Cooper as a separate character so that he isn't consumed by the entity that he created or vice versa. Alice Cooper combined morbid theatrics with Rock&Roll & the world was ready to eat it up. Alice Cooper made it big in a way that is difficult to understand now. I first saw Alice Cooper on the Muppet Show in a Devil costume, surrounded by monsters & was totally entranced. Alice Cooper presents this goofy, theatrical, shock via horror aesthetic, almost Vaudevillian show that mixes perfectly with Halloween delivered in a Rock&Roll package.

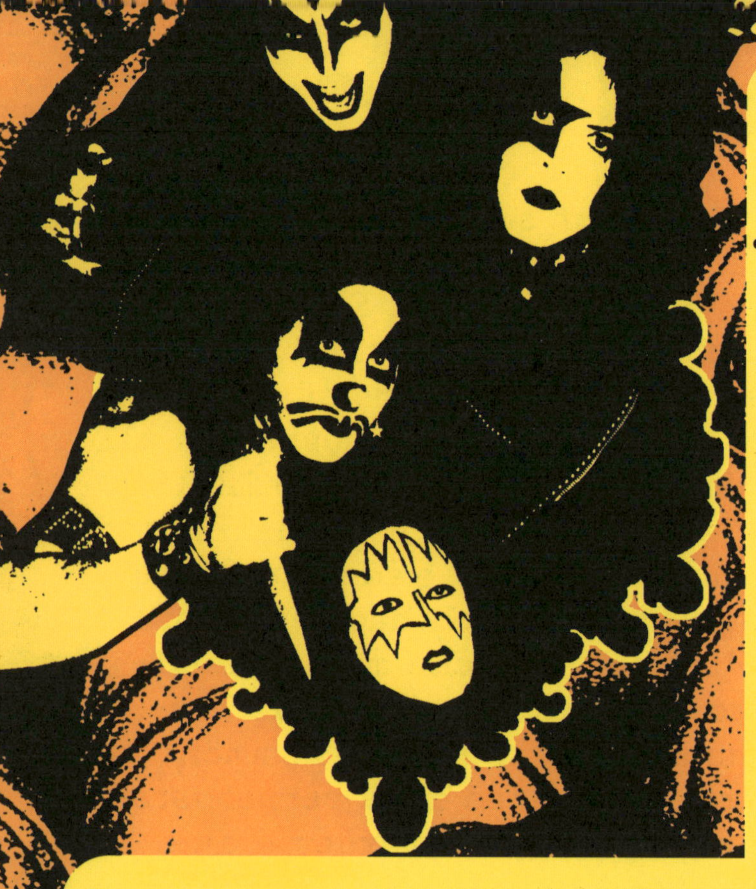

KISS

A carnival ride of a band, putting Rock&Roll on the lunchboxes of America's children. KISS started in 1974 in New York, by Gene Simmons & Paul Stanley, Ace Frehley & Peter Criss. Inspired by & taking their name from The New York Dolls, KISS managed to take Glam into the mainstream without mainstream support. Ignored by the critics, KISS used the aspects of Rock&Roll that attracted the common person to the genre: loud music, bombast & escapism to achieve massive success. One of the common things about a lot of these icons is that they were inspired by horror movies & comic books. KISS is no different, Bass player & founding member Gene Simmons ran & contributed to numerous comic book & science fiction fanzines & famously said "I was never interested in being a rock star. I always wanted to be Boris Karloff."

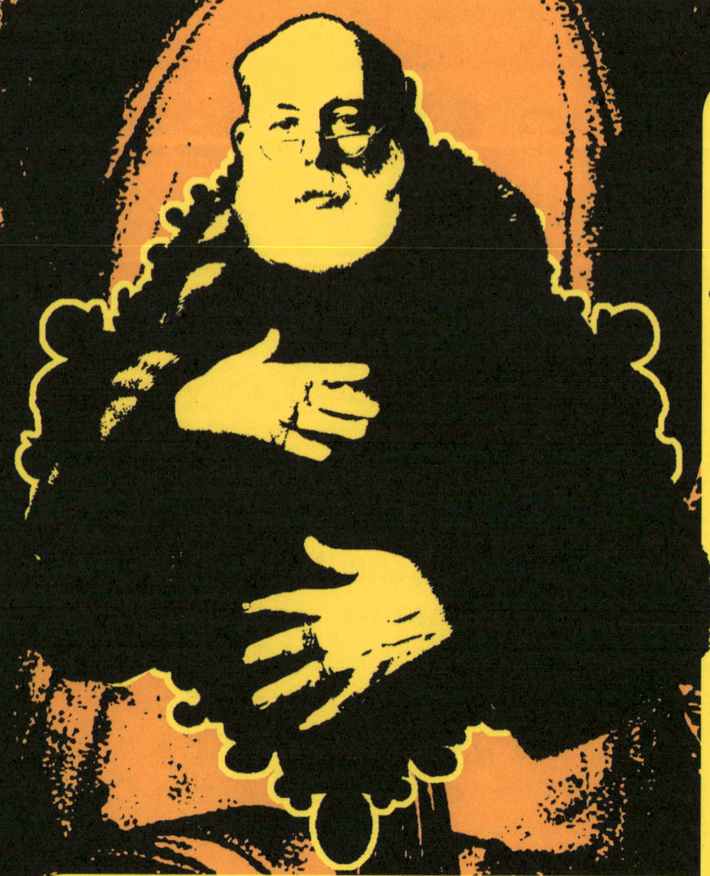

Edward Gorey

An eccentric artist of morbid masterpieces, Edward Gorey was an artist that was born in Chicago, Illinois. Gorey illustrated countless books (including the fantastic children's novels of John Bellairs which everyone should have read), book covers, wrote over one hundred books & even designed his own stage production of the classsic 1924 version of Dracula in his own distinct style. Gorey's art was dominated by a morbid sense of humor, a Victorian & Edwardian sensibility & intense cross-hatching, it is immediately recognizable. He also did the introduction for the PBS show "Mystery" which was hosted by Vincent Price. Besides being an accomplished artist Gorey also attended every performance of the New York Ballet for 25 years & would appear in public wearing furs, leading many people to think he was European.

Elvira

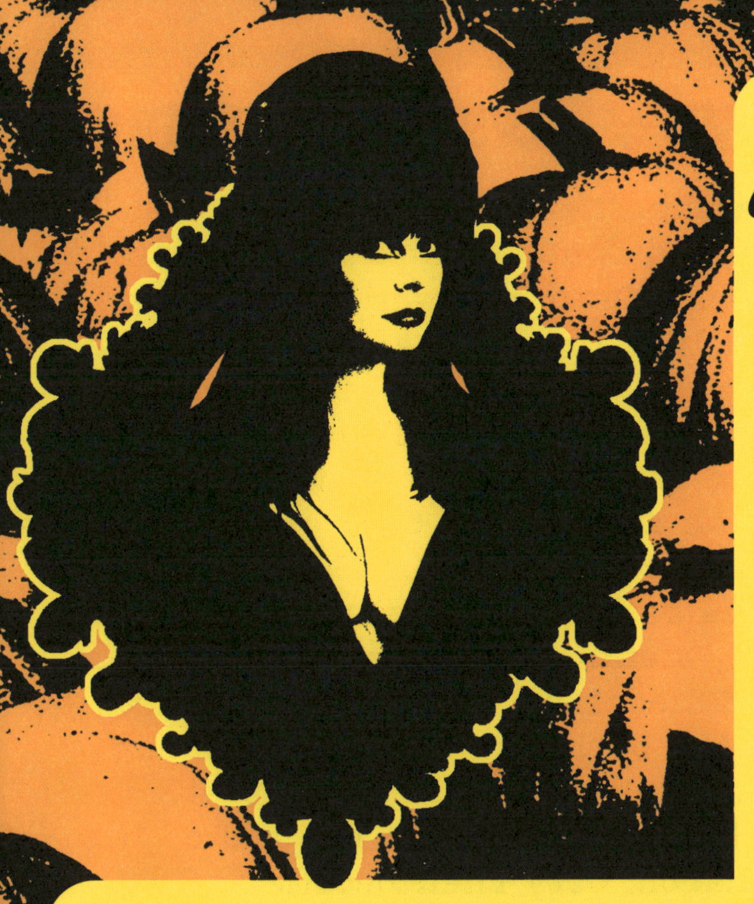

The host with the most! Born Cassandra Peterson, she began her show business journey as a showgirl in Las Vegas. Cassandra developed the base of the character Elvira as part of the legendary comedy group "The Groundlings" (which also spawned Pee-Wee Herman) in the 1970s. In the 80s, Elvira started out as a Horror movie host on late night TV for the show "Fright Night", but the character exploded & took off like a pair of pumpkins, rolling down a hill. Elvira has sold beer, had her own comic book, movie, pinball game, video game & more, all while promoting the goofier side of Horror. Her movie, "Elvira, Mistress of the Dark" is fun because it presents Elvira as a bad influence on an uptight town of squares. She eventually wins the town over but not before they try to burn her at the stake as a witch! Anyhow, it's good that she wins in the end showing that the true Halloween can triumph!

Glenn Danzig

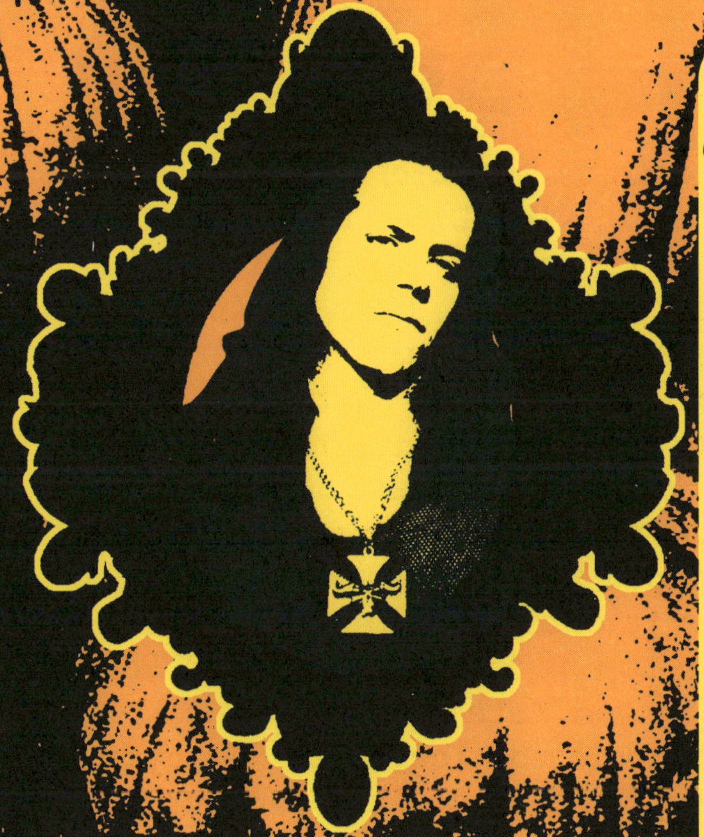

The Bad Boy, B-Movie based Baritone; Glenn Danzig was born Glenn Allen Anzalone in New Jersey in 1955. As a founder of the second-wave Punk band "The Misfits" he brought the Horror aspect to the fore in the early 1980s. Importantly, The Misfits brought a B-Movie sensibility with them & KISS aspect that didn't take itself too seriously. Danzig has always cut an imposing image that people have been intimidated by & this has gotten translated into the idea that he is overly serious. However, he just takes what he does seriously because he has fought for his whole life to bring his ideas into reality for all of humanity to enjoy! After the Misfits, Glenn moved on to start his heavier band Samhain (Celtic Halloween) which eventually turned into Danzig so he could be captain of his ship. Like a lot of the profiled people here he loved comics so he started his own comic company.

Ozzy Osbourne

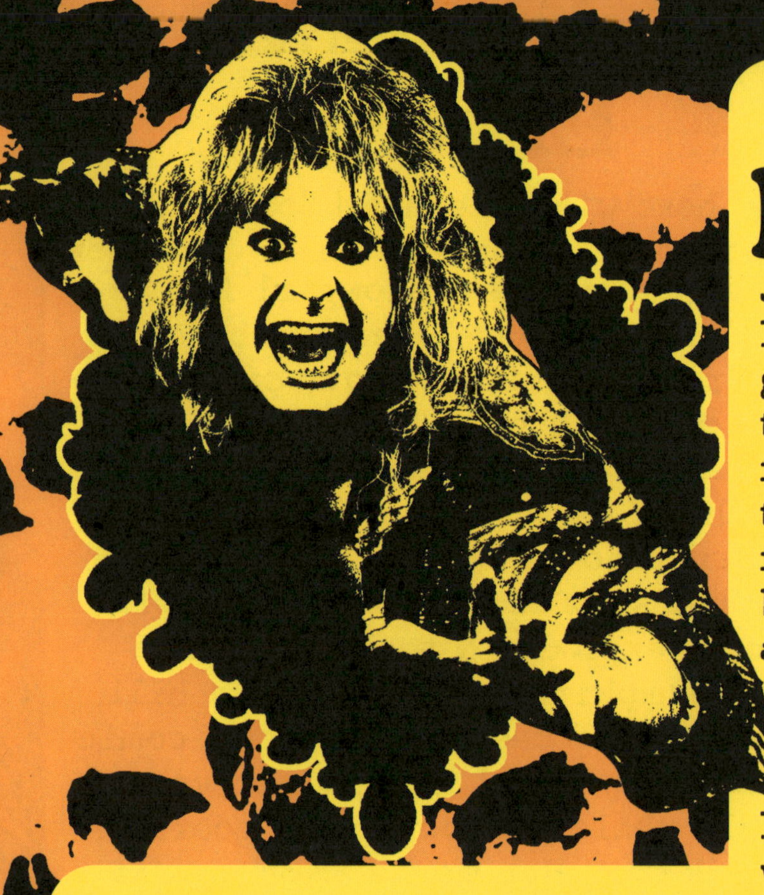

Keeping Metal dangerous in a world that tries to keep it safe. John "Ozzy" Osbourne was born in England in 1948. Ozzy had a difficult time growing up which gives him a sensitive side as a successful adult, that his fans can read. Inspired by the Beatles to become a musician, Ozzy eventually formed Black Sabbath in 1969. Black Sabbath was basically the first Heavy Metal band, blending the darker side of the Psychedelic Rock of the late sixties with both occult & drop out subjects. Ozzy was fired from Sabbath in 1979 & he went solo with the aid of his wife Sharon. Ozzy then became infamous for biting the head off a bat during a show. In the 90s Ozzy introduced lots of new Metal acts with his Ozzfest series then introduced himself to a whole new set of fans with "The Osbournes" reality show. Ozzy has shown the ability to survive & adapt yet stay the same at the core.

King Diamond

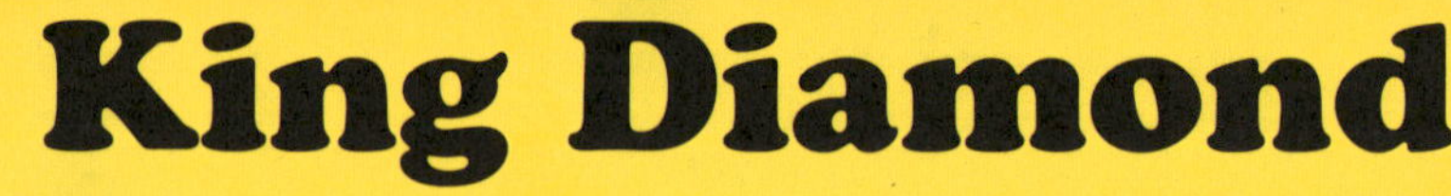

Operatic, bombastic, metallic, epic & Satanic. King Diamond brought the Halloween factor to the fore into the world of 1980s metal. Born as Kim Petersen in Denmark, King Diamond has delivered in his signature falsetto, horror stories in the vehicle of Thrash Metal. King Diamond combined the shock rock stage show & makeup of Alice Cooper with the makeup of KISS but made it entirely his own, putting it all on top of Prog influenced 1980s Thrash-tinged Metal. His other well-known band is the legendary Mercyful Fate. King Diamond writes concept albums that tell an entire story through the songs, his stage show then elaborates on these stories with Diamond playing the role of the storyteller & the protagonist. King Diamond sings into a microphone that is affixed to crossed bones like some kind of unsettled grave digger.

Tim Burton

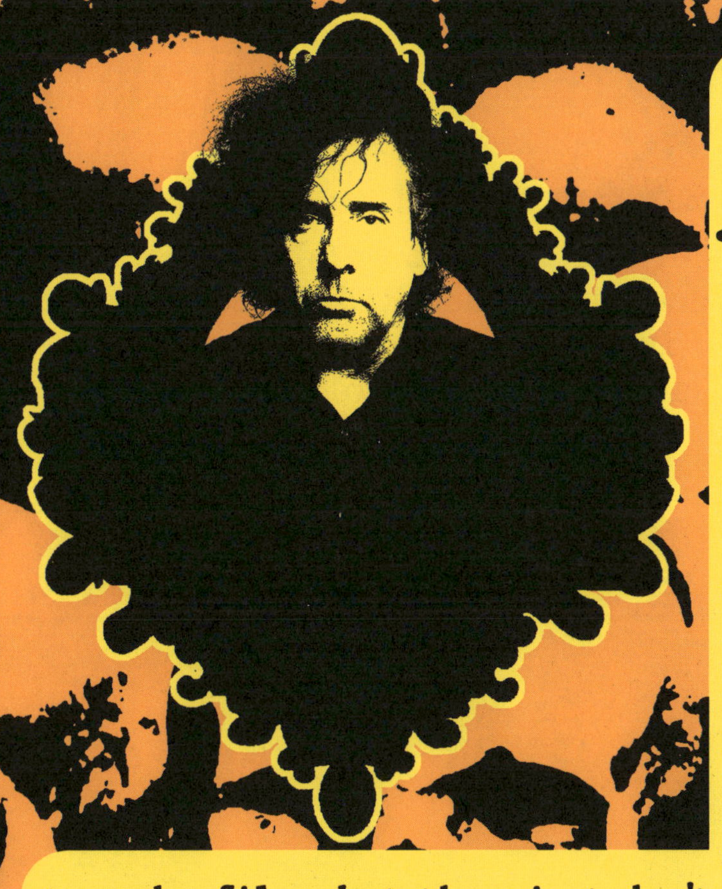

An Auteur of suburban weirdness, Tim Burton is an American film-maker that has brought more eccentric strangeness to the screen than any of his contemporaries. Born in Burbank, CA, Burton is a product of the TV world that surrounded & stimulated him. Burton was so bored by reality, he created a world of weirdness to escape into. Luckily for us, he shared that world. Burton released his first full-length "Pee-Wee's Big Adventure" (check out Pee-wee's Halloween appearances on Letterman) & knocked out a series of classics before he burned through his childhood inspiration in 2001. Burton has continued to make films but they just don't compare. Burton followed Pee-Wee with "Beetlejuice", a ghost story told from the perspective of ghosts. Burton used Oingo Boingo frontman Danny Elfman to score so many of his movies that they just seemed to go together & defined each other.

Marilyn Manson

Bringing the spooky into the 90s & beyond. Marilyn Manson was born Brian Warner in Ohio but came up in Florida. By the time the 90s came around you had to do a lot more to shock the world. This was a time when world-weariness & been there, done that attitutes were trendy, so Manson had to go harder than anyone previous. What worked for Alice Cooper & the like was known & considered corny & the world already had the advent of every kind of extreme music from Grind Core to Gangster Rap. I was really into old Punk when Marilyn Manson first emerged & his "Spooky Kid" followers were looked down on by subcultural purists of the time, I think mostly because of Manson's success at bringing in a new audience. All that said, Manson is centrally an interesting artist that has been able to successfully communicate his own brand of morbidity to the public.

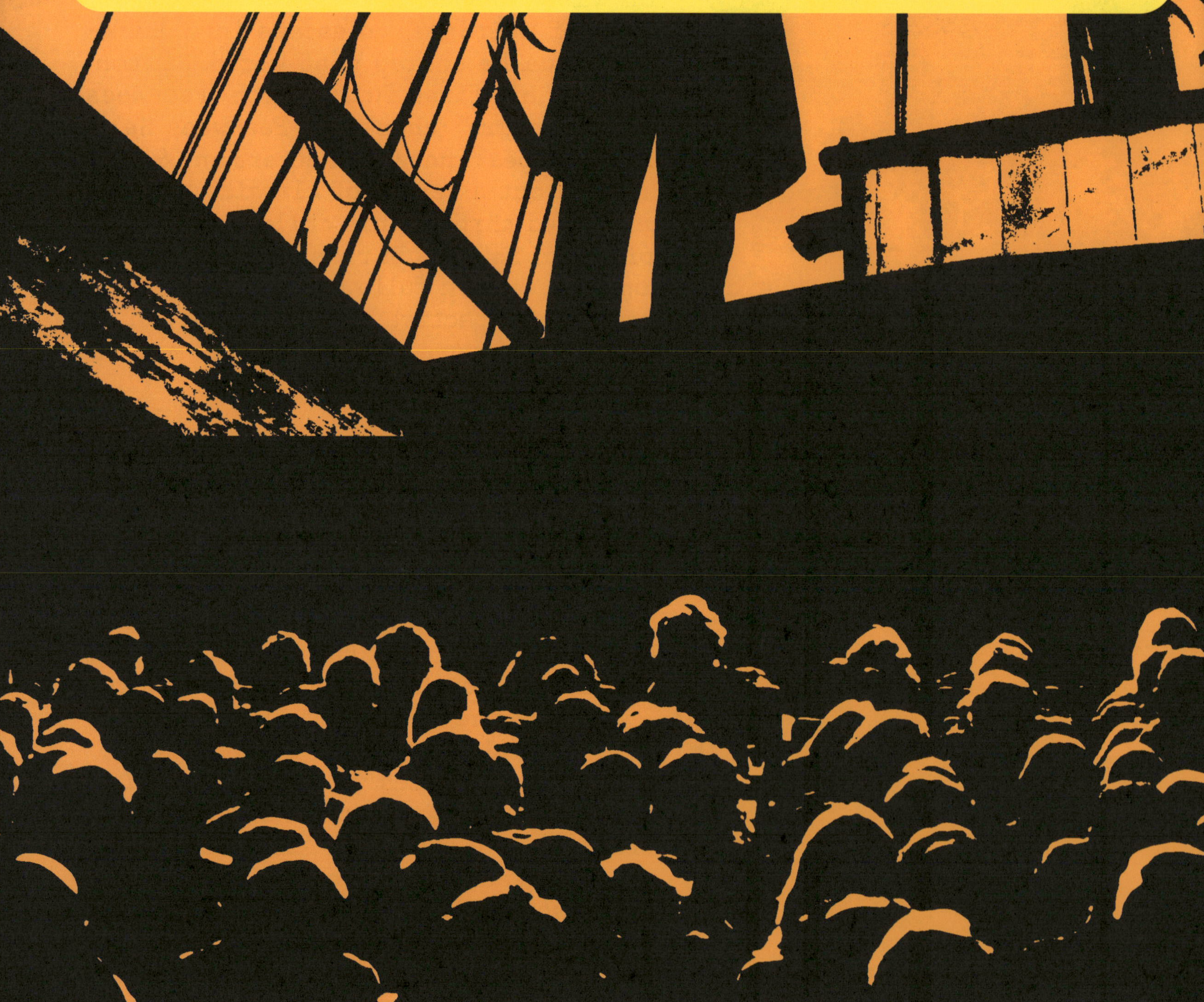

Movies

Movies help us understand reality & unreality. They're summations of the human soul. Movies have a way of condensing ideas, moods, themes, what have you into a tidy package. Served with buttery popcorn they are perfect! The right selection of Halloween movies get us ready for Halloween.

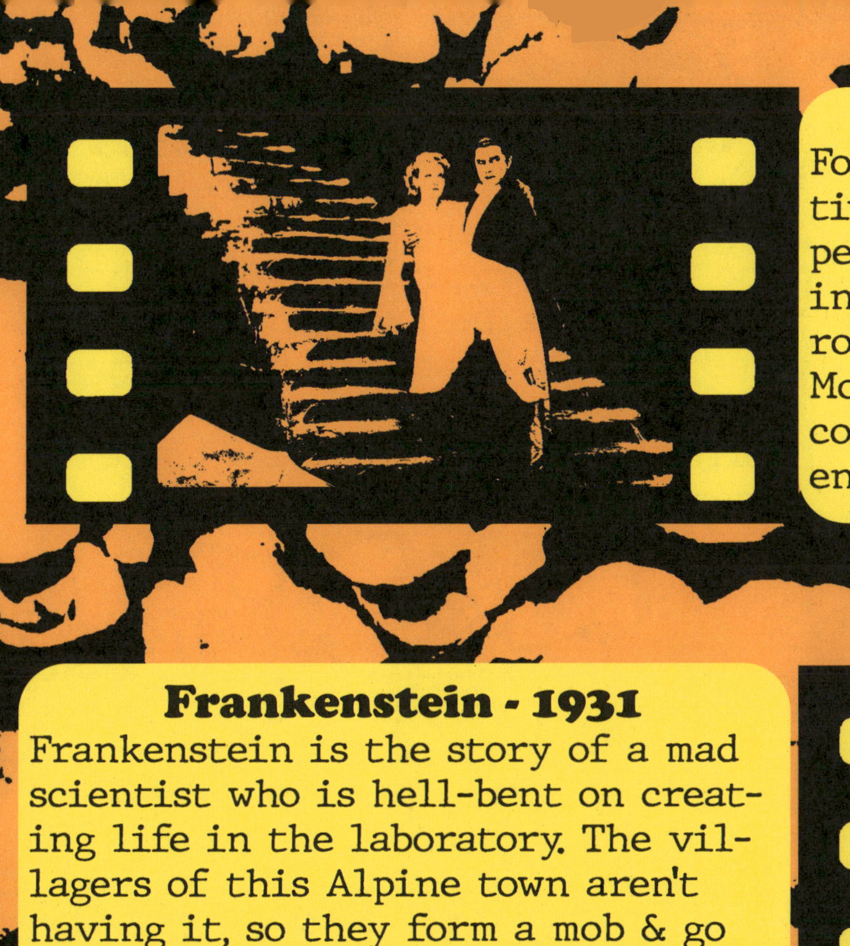

Dracula - 1931

Following Bela Lugosi as the seductive Vampire Count Dracula. Lugosi perfected the role on Broadway originally & it would be his defining role. Dracula went on to shape the Monster Movie genre for decades to come as a Gothic Horror piece influenced by German Expressionist Film.

Frankenstein - 1931

Frankenstein is the story of a mad scientist who is hell-bent on creating life in the laboratory. The villagers of this Alpine town aren't having it, so they form a mob & go after the both of them. The story is a perfect metaphor for humanity's relationship to their own creations.

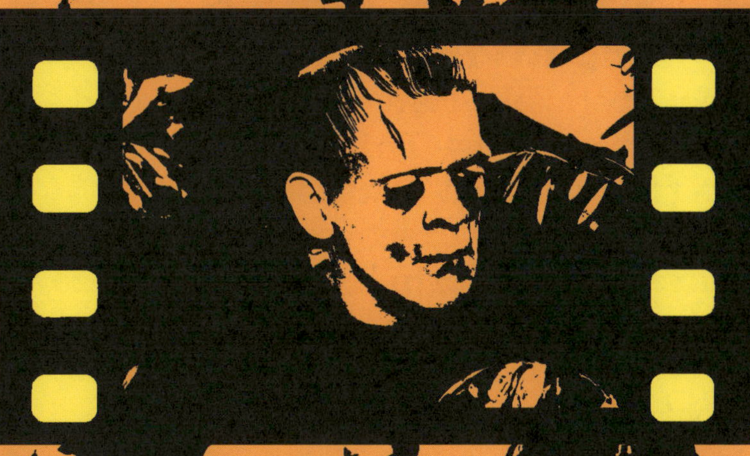

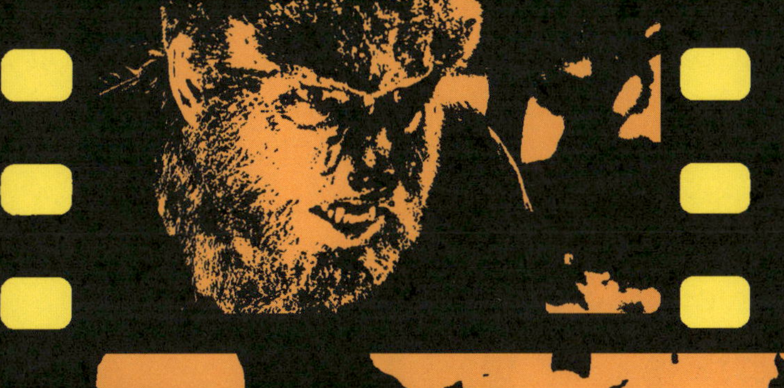

The Wolf Man - 1941

The Wolf Man tells the story of a man (Lon Chaney Jr.) who has received the curse of the werewolf! Even though I like to imagine all these movies taking place in the same Transylvanian locale, this one takes place in Wales.

The Creature From The Black Lagoon - 1954

The Creature From The Black Lagoon follows a group of scientists who are travelling down the Amazon to find this prehistoric creature. The creature falls in love with the lady scientist & will stop at nothing to get her! Originally released in 3D!

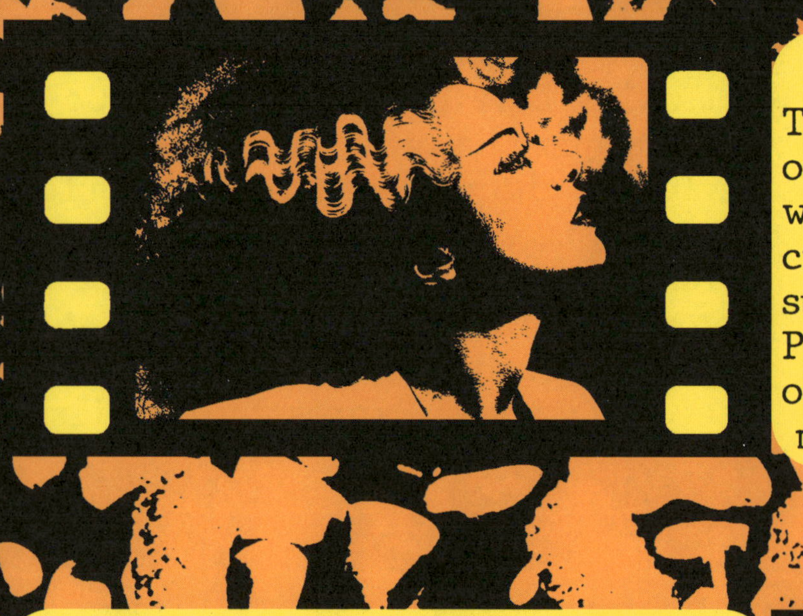

Bride of Frankenstein · 1935

The "reformed" Dr. Frankenstein is outdone by his mentor, Dr. Pretorius who has been experimenting with creating life. Dr. Frankenstein's monster turns up & wants a bride, Dr. Pretorious is more than willing to oblige. Una O'connor plays a house marm who steals the show!

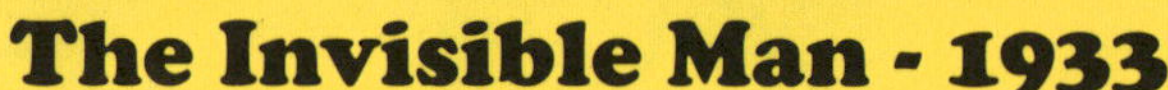

The Invisible Man · 1933

The Invisible Man is another Mad Scientist story. This time, Dr. Jack Griffin (played fantastically by Claude Rains) discovers the chemical secret of invisibility that is also driving him crazy. A mad scientist driven madder by his invisibility potion? Mayhem ensues.

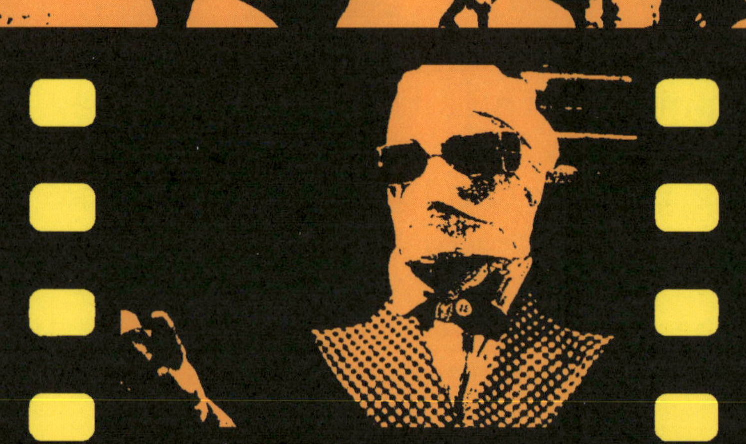

The Mummy · 1932

Boris Karloff stars in the title role. This movie is kind of a meditation on the subject of Egyptology. It touches on the plunder of Egypt by colonial powers & the lurking strength of the Egyptian Empire which is just waiting to exact its revenge on said plunderers.

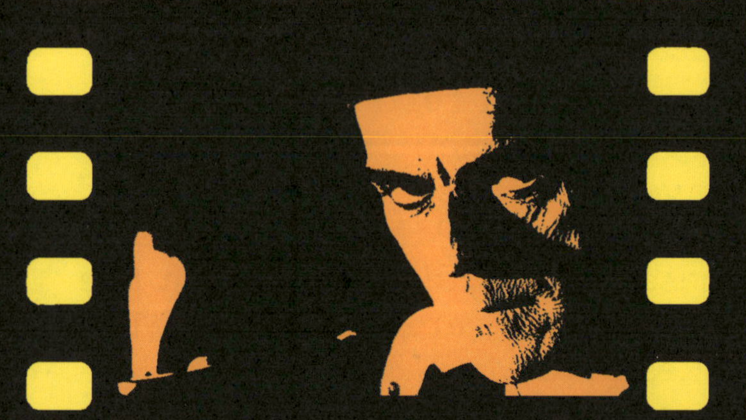

Abbott & Costello Meet Frankenstein · 1948

By the time that 1948 rolled around, the Universal Monsters had been absorbed into the pop culture & were ready to be incorporated into the comedic stylings of Bud Abbott & Lou Costello. This movie still makes me laugh when I watch it, which is more than I can say for most movies.

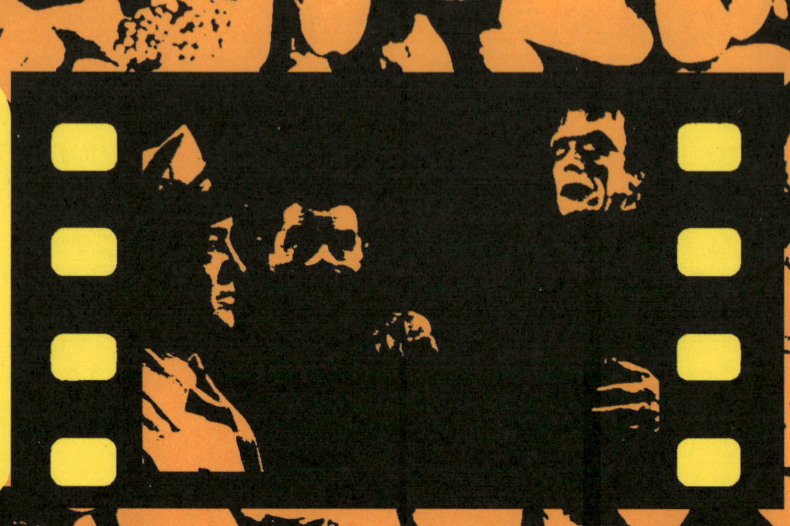

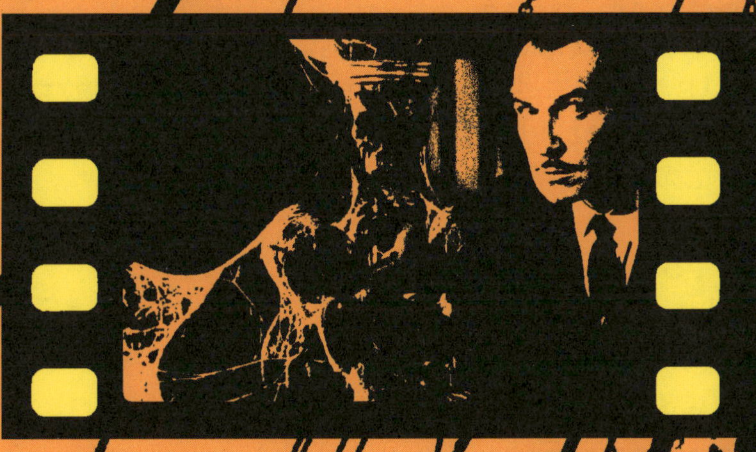

House on Haunted Hill - 1959

Vincent Price stars as the eccentric millionaire host of a Haunted House Party designed to weed out the party-goers leaving the lone survivor as a winner of a bunch of cash. The morbid sense of humor is fantastic as are the haunted house props that are used to terrorize the guests.

Dracula - 1958

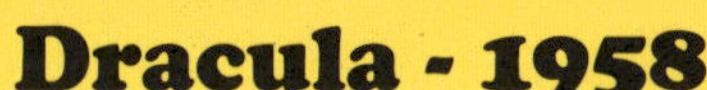

Christopher Lee plays Dracula in this update with Peter Cushing as Van Helsing. I love the Hammer Horror movies in general, they capture the Gothic Horror genre perfectly. Hammer Horror brought new blood to the genre when they desperately needed it!

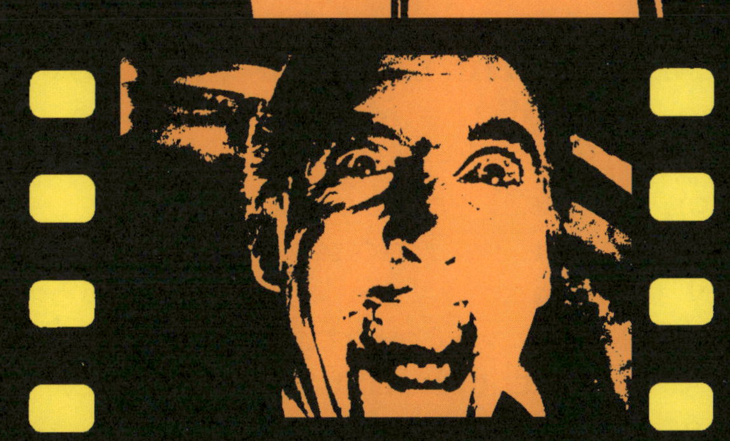

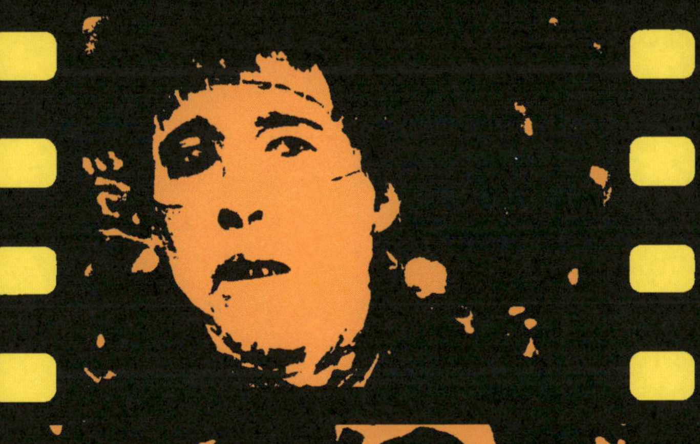

The Curse of Frankenstein - 1957

Peter Cushing plays Dr. Frankenstein & Christopher Lee plays his monster in the Hammer take on the classic. One thing I really dig about these movies is that they set a totally new tone for the classic Universal series. Hammer Horror is bright, technicolor & bold!

Mad Monster Party? - 1967

This Rankin/Bass stop-motion movie was written by MAD magazine creator Harvey Kurtzman, characters designed by Jack Davis & starring Boris Karloff & Phyllis Diller! All the monsters are invited to the Isle of Evil for their convention & the head to pass the crown to his nephew.

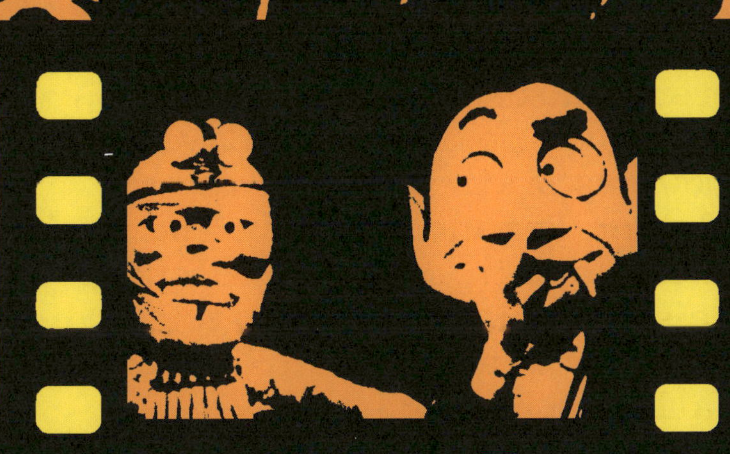

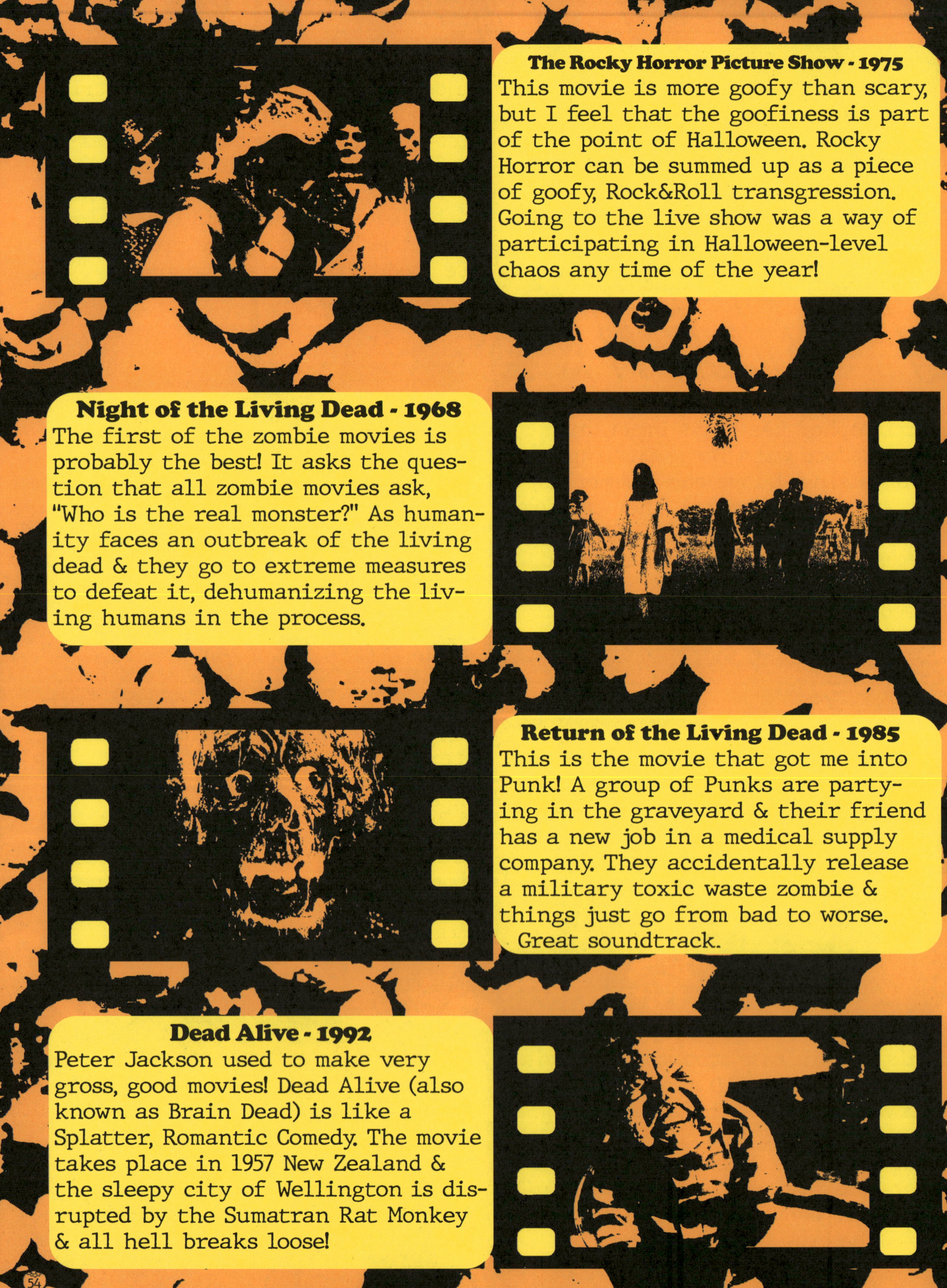

The Rocky Horror Picture Show - 1975

This movie is more goofy than scary, but I feel that the goofiness is part of the point of Halloween. Rocky Horror can be summed up as a piece of goofy, Rock&Roll transgression. Going to the live show was a way of participating in Halloween-level chaos any time of the year!

Night of the Living Dead - 1968

The first of the zombie movies is probably the best! It asks the question that all zombie movies ask, "Who is the real monster?" As humanity faces an outbreak of the living dead & they go to extreme measures to defeat it, dehumanizing the living humans in the process.

Return of the Living Dead - 1985

This is the movie that got me into Punk! A group of Punks are partying in the graveyard & their friend has a new job in a medical supply company. They accidentally release a military toxic waste zombie & things just go from bad to worse. Great soundtrack.

Dead Alive - 1992

Peter Jackson used to make very gross, good movies! Dead Alive (also known as Brain Dead) is like a Splatter, Romantic Comedy. The movie takes place in 1957 New Zealand & the sleepy city of Wellington is disrupted by the Sumatran Rat Monkey & all hell breaks loose!

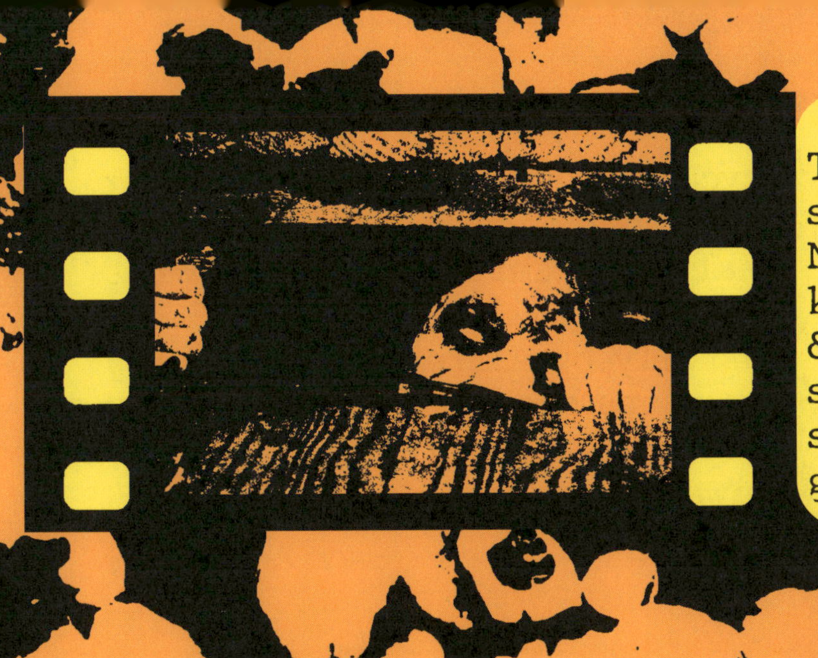

Evil Dead - 1981

The beginning of the Evil Dead series & the introduction of the Necronomicon to the masses! College kids go visit a cabin in the woods & discover that the owner was researching something evil which is summoned from beyond! The series gets sillier as it goes on.

House - 1986

House tells the tale of an author who has a run of bad luck who moves into his Aunt's house which turns out to be haunted! Filled with hilarious encounters with a variety of monstrous abominations that are determined to get this house clear of all inhabitants!

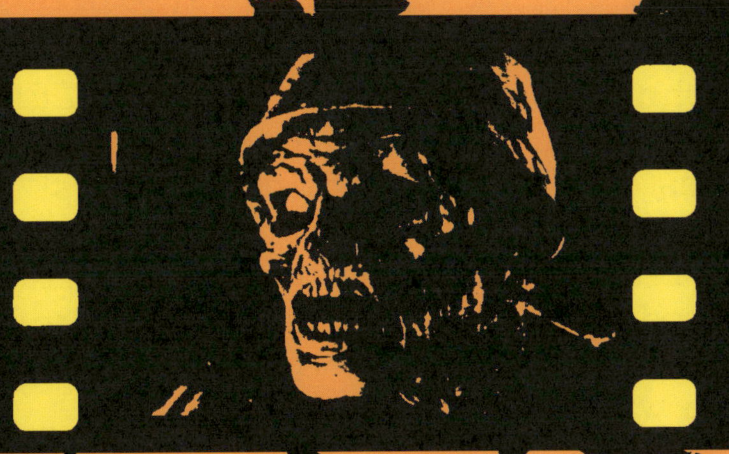

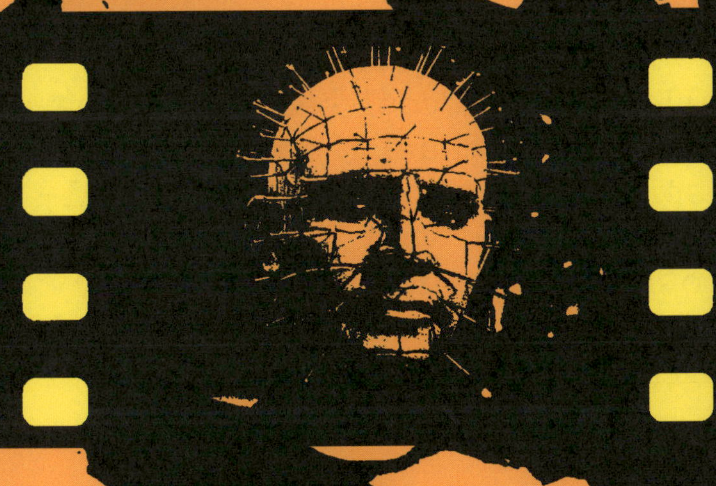

Hellraiser - 1987

Hellraiser is the first in a series of movies about sado-masochistic demons that are summoned by a mysterious puzzlebox, curiousity & desire. Hellraiser owes a lot to the horror pulps that then became the common language of horror movies!

Beetlejuice - 1988

Beetlejuice is a ghost story told from the perspective of the ghosts. A couple dies & is stuck in their house which is purchased by annoying New Yorkers. The ghost couple get desperate & accidentally summon the "bio-exorcist" Beetlejuice who they then have to get rid of.

Psycho - 1960

Psycho might be the first Slasher movie, but it also the first psycho-analytical thriller, asking "What makes the killer tick?" Handled masterfully by Alfred Hitchcock, Psycho paves the way for the Slasher as main character movies of the 80s & onwards.

Halloween - 1978

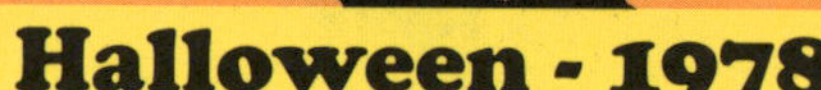

John Carpenter wrote, directed & did the music for this masterpiece. The unstoppable psycho Michael Myers escapes from a mental institution & returns to the scene of his child-hood crime to kill again! The town has cast Myers as the Boogie Man & he wreaks havoc on Halloween.

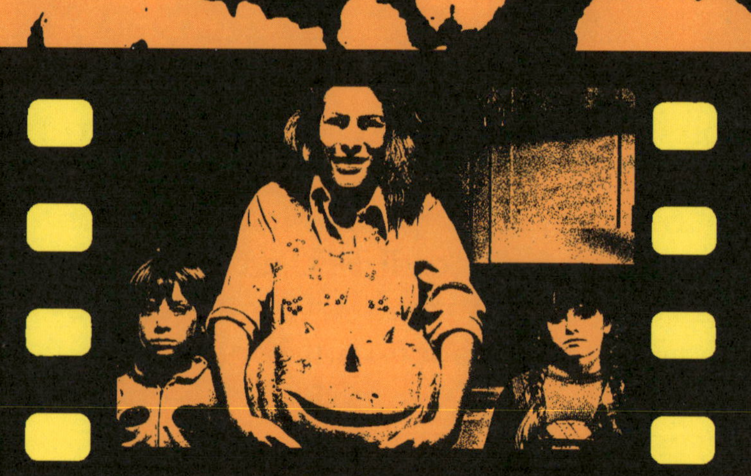

Halloween 3 - 1982

Halloween 3 is cool because it leaves the whole Michael Myers story alone & spins an entirely different Halloween themed yarn. This one is about a shadowy novelty company that has an ulterior motive in selling Halloween masks to the kids!

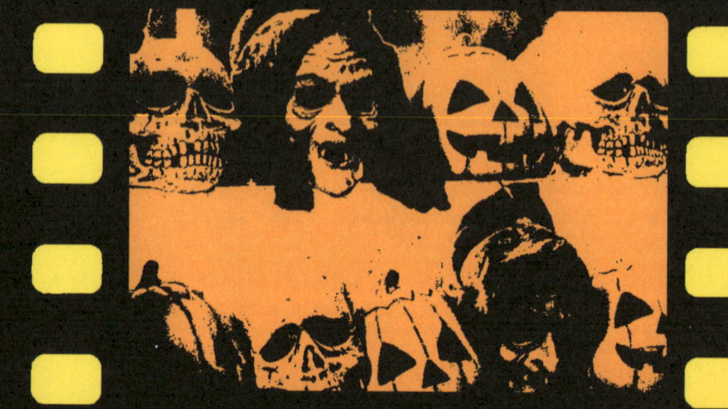

The Shining - 1980

This manages to be one of the scariest Horror movies of all time, directed by the great Stanley Kubrick. Jack Nicholson takes his wife & son to write his book in a haunted hotel & he goes nuts! Excellent performances by everyone, from a book by Stephen King.

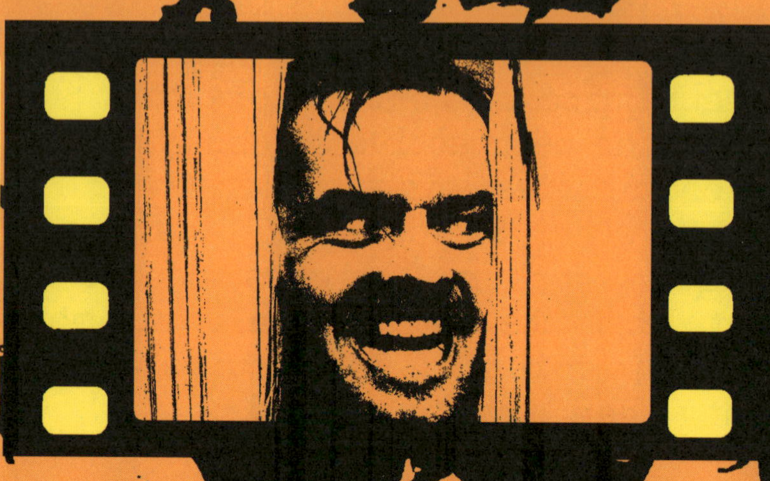

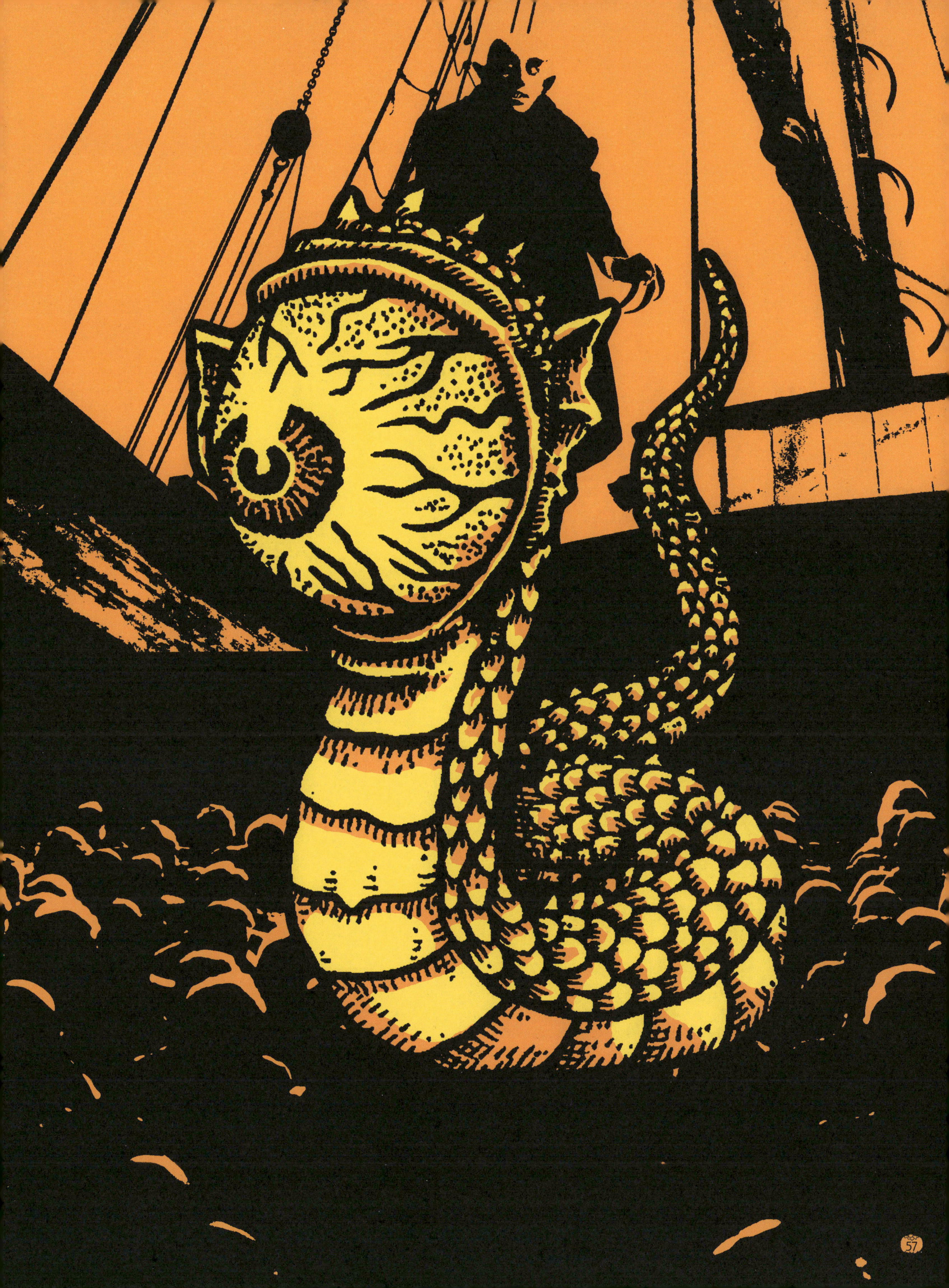

Music

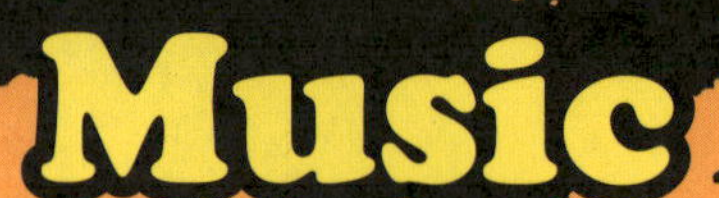

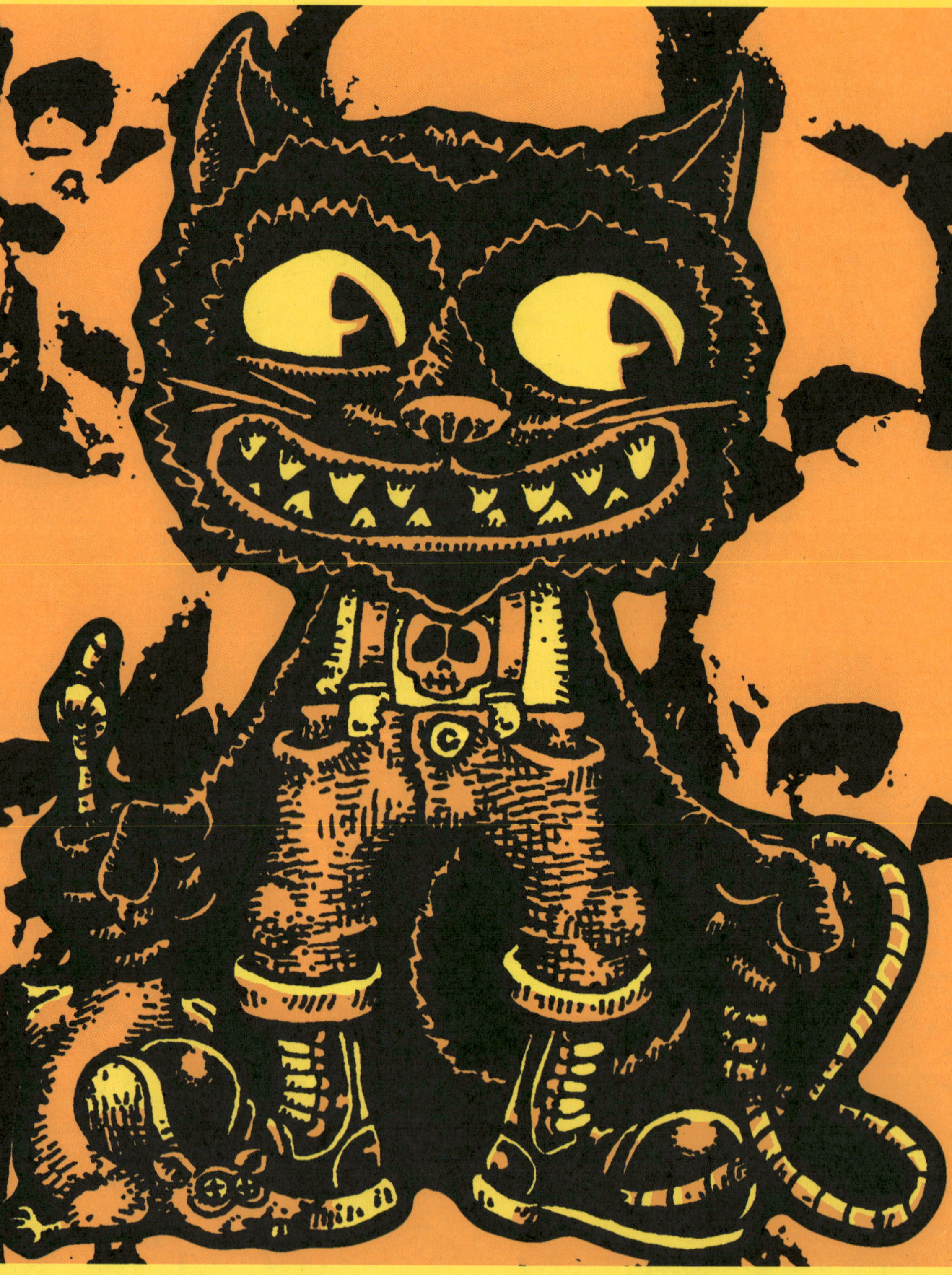

Music has long been a world where aspects of Halloween could hide. These are the "Dress Up" & "Be Yourself" parts of the holiday. Our society has progressed beyond that, but, you have to remember that Rock&Roll was called the "Devil's Music" not that long ago. Before that it was the "jungle drums" of Jazz. Even dancing has been considered a gateway to possession by some. These are the territories of Racism & Religion, philosophies of the Dark Ages that I don't touch.

Screamin' Jay Hawkins

Aspiring Opera singer Screamin' Jay Hawkins drunkenly manifested people's fears about "Race Music" being an entry point for African Demons disrupting the starchy surface of American life. Screamin' Jay played the role of witch doctor that is implied by the music but hadn't been articulated up to that point. Besides dressing up in the part he would put on shows using coffins, snakes & the other tools of the trade.

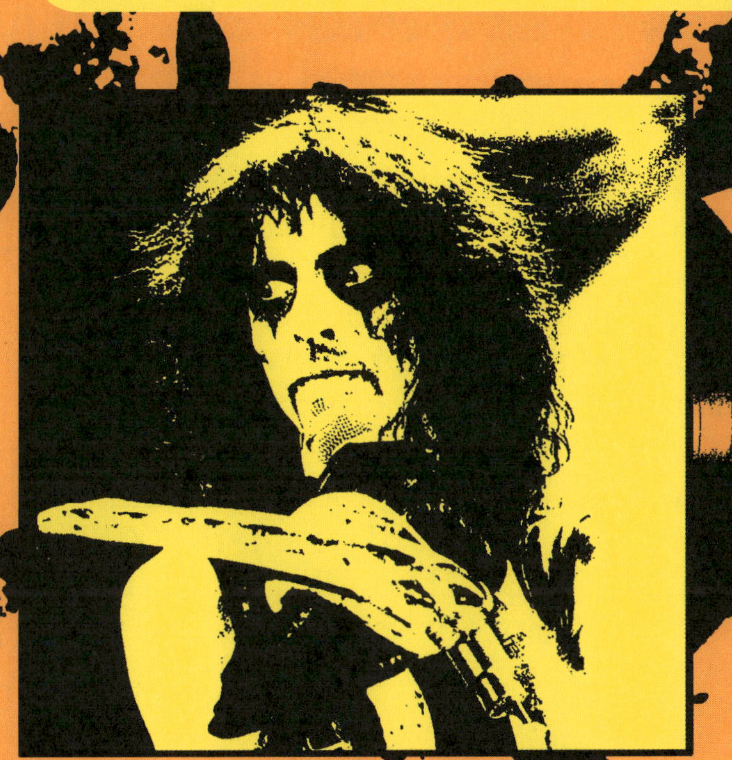

Alice Cooper

Alice Cooper is the Edgar Allan Poe of Rock&Roll. No other artist has so singularly defined themselves with the macabre & if they've come close, they're totally influenced by him. While this was packaged as "Shock Rock" in the past, I think his show is more Vaudeville than the moving target that is genuinely shocking an audience. What you get in addition to this great image & show is a genuine talent & great tunes too!

David Bowie

While David Bowie wasn't outwardly spooky or morbid, he did create a character for his 1974 Diamond Dogs album & tour called Halloween Jack. I would argue that Bowie has included bizarre & morbid subjects throughout his career & he did popularize theatricality in music. So, again while Bowie shouldn't be thought of directly with Halloween, there is a lot there in terms of indirect influence on Halloween.

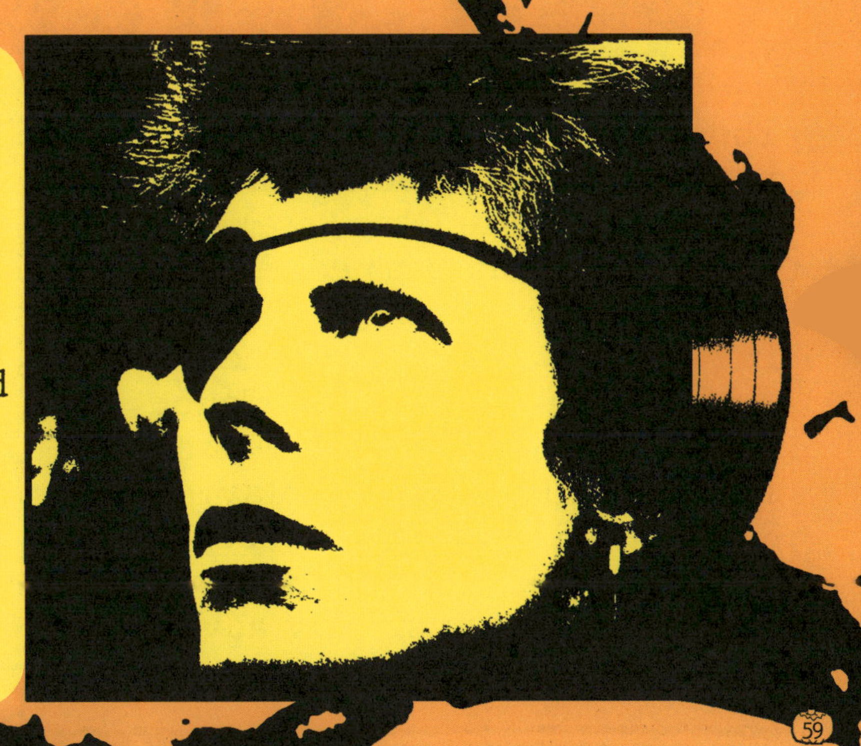

Black Sabbath

Their name says it all, implying a Witch's Sabbath & was directly lifted from a Boris Karloff movie title. Birmingham, England's Black Sabbath was the first Heavy Metal band. Taking note that people lined up to see horror movies, they decided to push the band in that direction. The band evoked so much darkness that they started to superstitiously wear crosses to ward off a curse placed on them by witches when they wouldn't play Stonehenge.

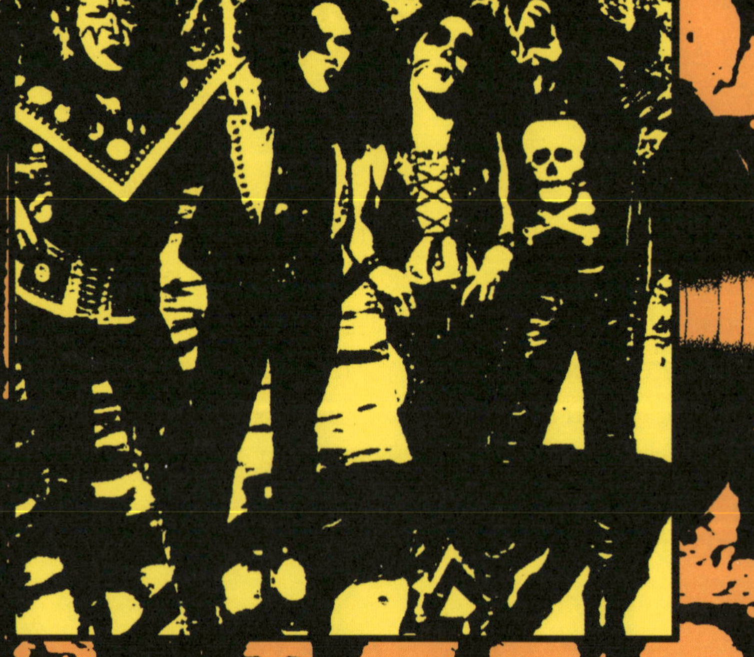

KISS

KISS started properly, four NYC guys that wanted to be the Beatles. Sometimes a limited budget, lots of drive & a vision gets the goods. The vision was provided by bass player Gene Simmons, combining horror movie, comic book & Rock&Roll imagery together. Proper Glam & Halloween is always more five & dime than VOGUE magazine. KISS, although predating Punk had a more manageable feeling than so many other bands of the 70s.

The Damned

The Damned have the honor of being the first English Punk band to release a single (New Rose) & album (Damned Damned Damned) & tour the states. Besides early Punk just having a Halloween feeling the Damned's singer Dave Vanian has a Count Dracula image & the band essentially birthed Hardcore by playing fast & intense & then Gothic Rock just by looking cool,adding keyboards & becoming more musically adventuresome over time.

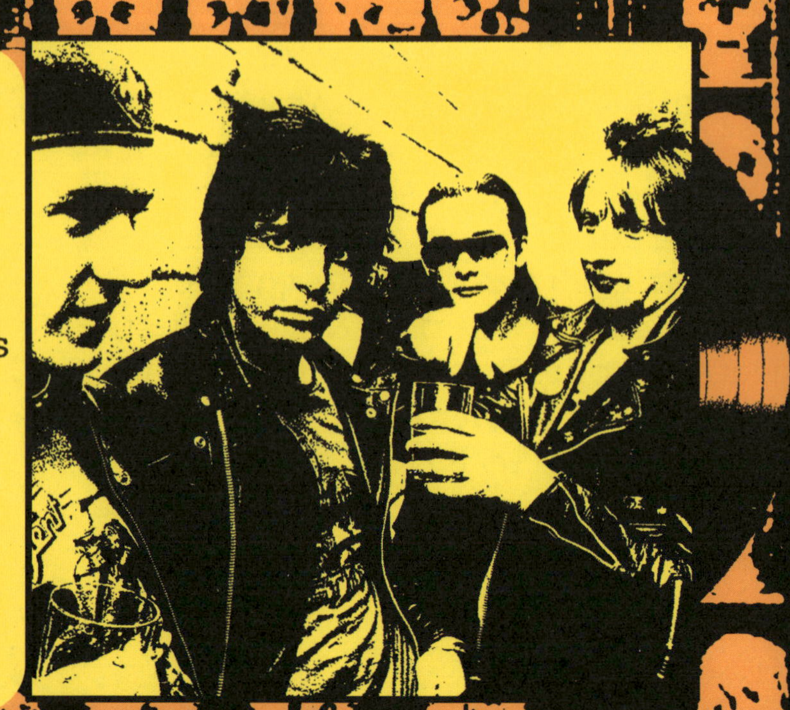

The Cramps

The Cramps came out of the early (1970s) Punk scene in NYC & have come to define a certain kind of Garage & Rockabilly Punk that still lives on. The Cramps embodied the Halloween element of old Rock&Roll. Lead by husband & wife team Lux Interior & Poison Ivy, the Cramps used horror movie themes & macabre lyrics to make an atmosphere that creates the Halloween mood that earned them a place on painted leathers & mixtapes for decades!

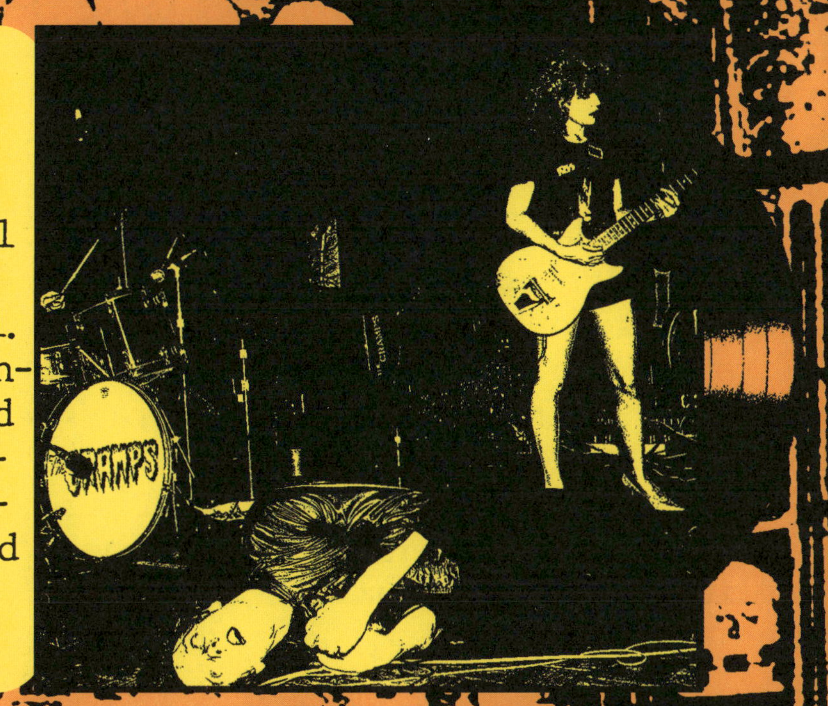

The Misfits

The Misfits applied the KISS theory of more bang for your buck to Punk Rock with consistent branding & b-movie horror imagery using the Crimson Ghost as their mascot & taking their name from Marilyn Monroe's final movie. Formed in Lodi, New Jersey 1977, the Misfits embraced the 2nd wave of Punk which was less artistic & more anti-social & obsessed with the spectacle & violence of the thing. The Misfits gave the audience what they wanted, hard!

Siouxsie & the Banshees

Siouxsie & the Banshees formed as part of the initial Punk explosion in the UK. Siouxsie was part of the Bromley Contingent that were the most infamous followers of the Sex Pistols. Siouxsie & the Banshees really found themselves as pioneers of Goth in the 80s. The band was musically adventuresome like most Post-Punk outfits. Siouxsie, taking her cues from the Femme Fatales of silent movies, made herself into an icon for eternity!

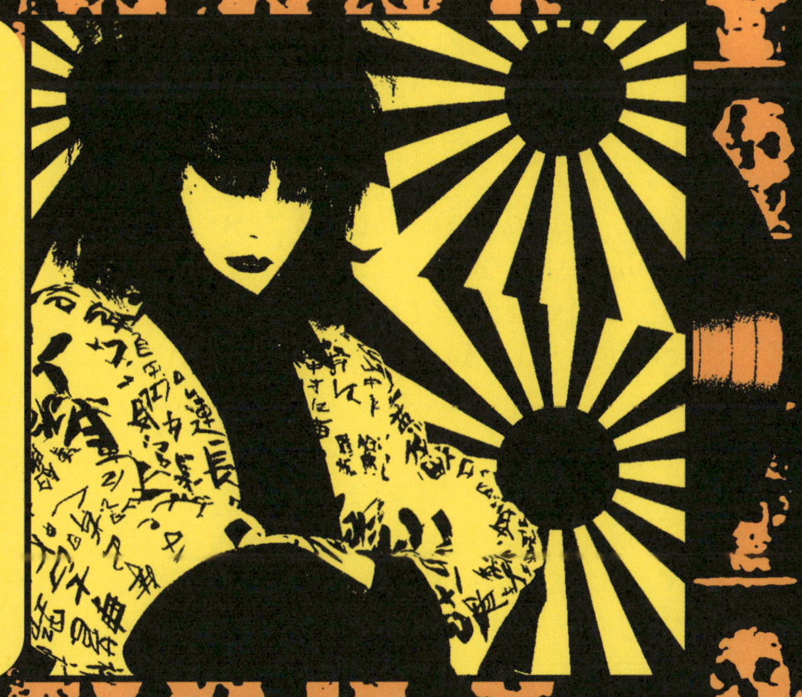

Bauhaus

Naming themselves after the German Art Group, England's Bauhaus codified what would become Gothic Rock. Slender, angular, sexy & cool, Bauhaus looked like a Bowie take on Vampires. The band's biggest song & first single was "Bela Lugosi's Dead" an over 9 minute epic Dub exploration. Like most Post-Punk, Bauhaus was musically adventurous, covering all the bases from Reggae to Psychedelic to Funk to Glam.

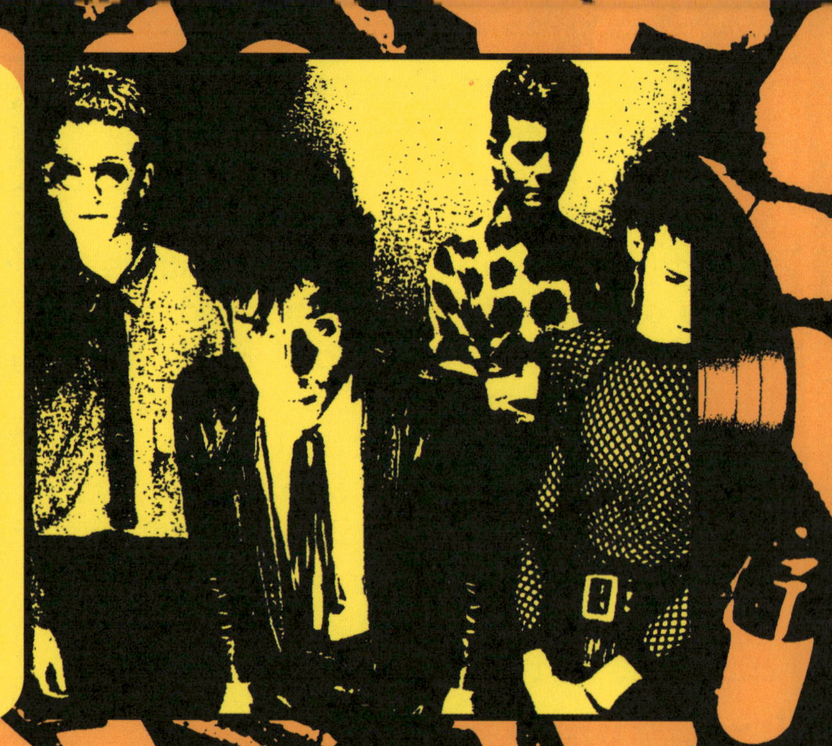

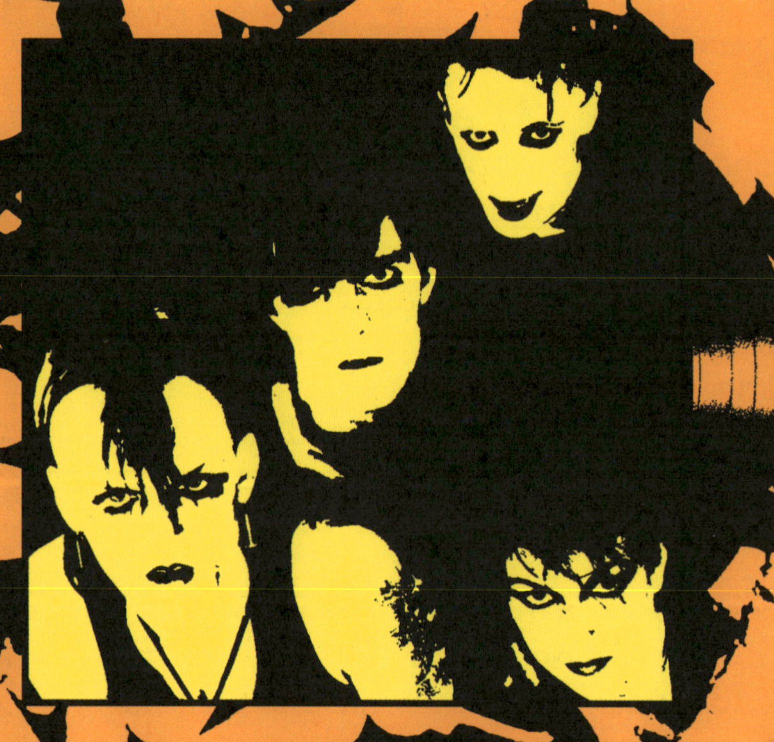

Alien Sex Fiend

England's Alien Sex Fiend took the Gothic imagery & sound that had been established up until that point & ran them through electronic machines making a Punky/junky sounding Electro-Goth that is still distinct in the world of music! Echoing the Cramps (And Goblinko) with a husband & wife team being the backbone of the band. Owing a lot to Jamaican Dub for their sound, Alien Sex Fiend also used lots of samples in their music.

Skinny Puppy

Canada's Skinny Puppy sounds like music made by Daleks. Embodying the part of Industrial music when you get your hand caught in the machine, Skinny Puppy have the ability to deliver soothing & disturbing sounds all in the same song. Industrial music was initially used to describe the sound of Iggy & the Stooges' Detroit Rock, but as Rock&Roll became more passe & electronic music came to the fore, Industrial has been keyboard driven.

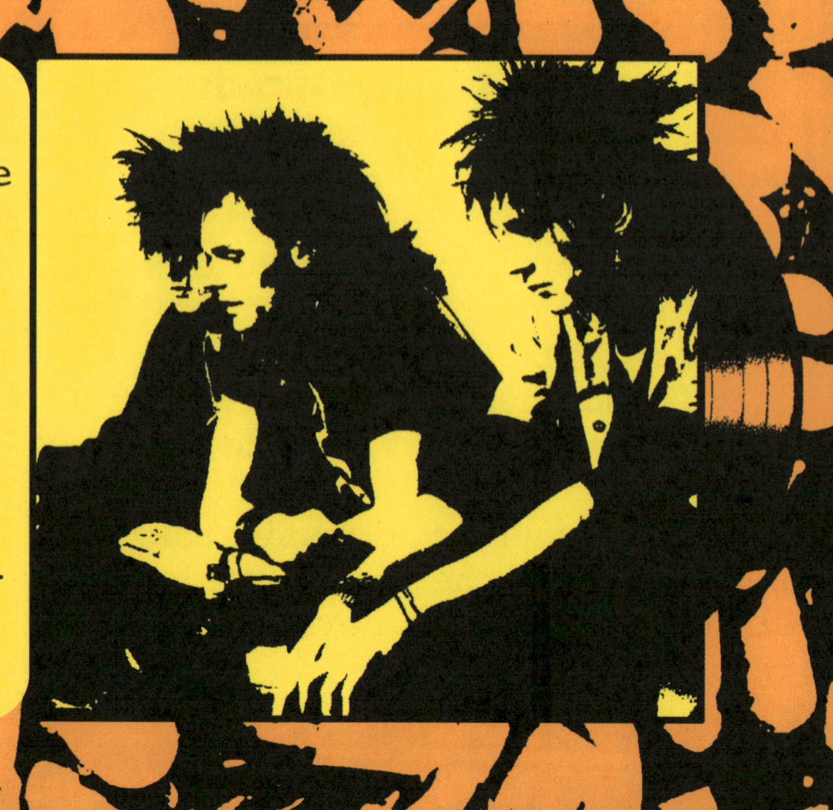

Nine Inch Nails

Goth & Industrial started to go mainstream in the 90s & we can blame Chicago's Nine Inch Nails & their catchy tunes for this! They had a bed made by Depeche Mode & countless other electro-pop acts, but NIN took electro & dragged it through the mud, which made it palatable to American Rock listeners who were more acclimated to the raw power of Rock&Roll & Heavy Metal which were becoming boring & predictable by this point (1988).

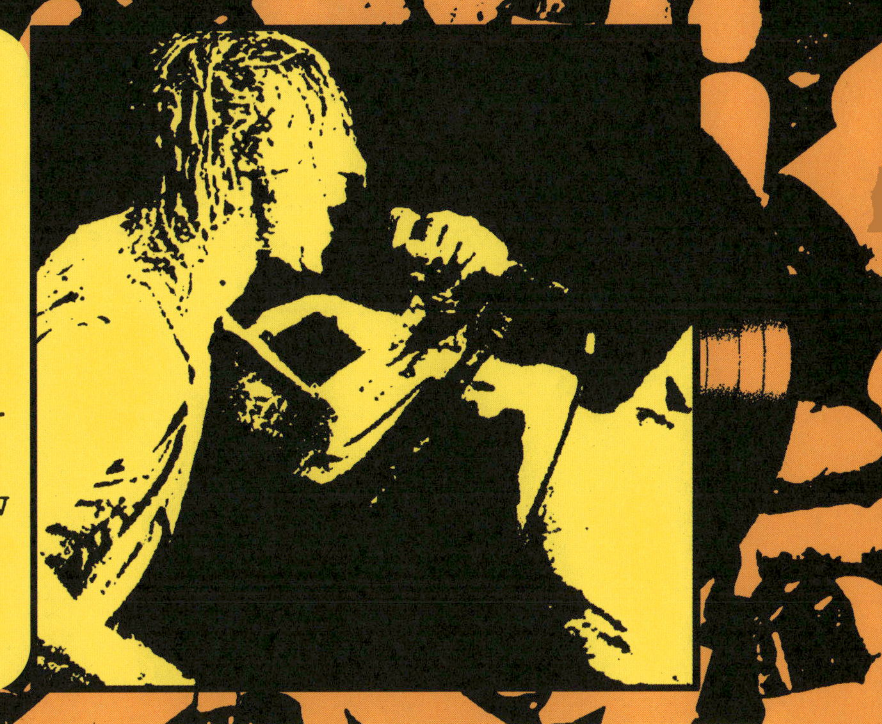

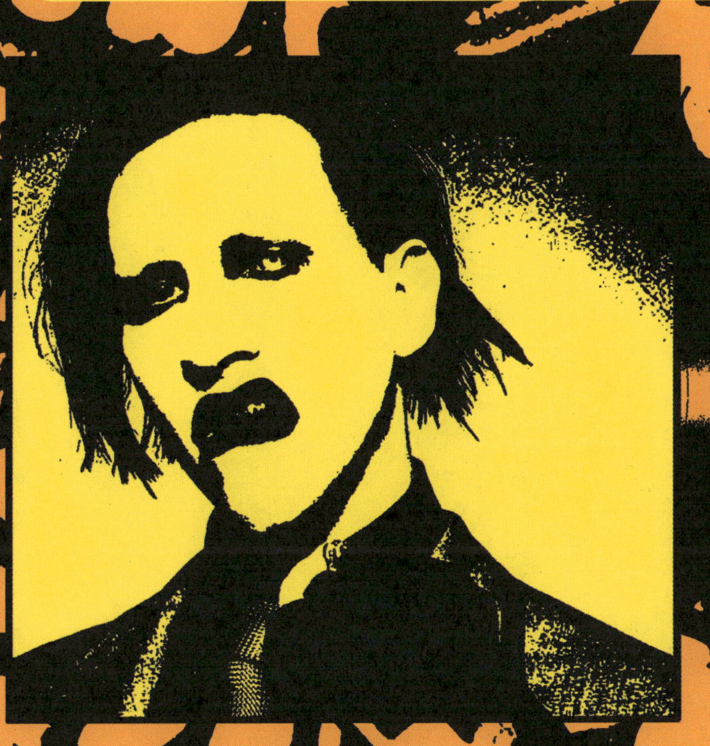

Marilyn Manson

Florida's Marilyn Manson took the popularity of Goth/Industrial Rock & welded it onto an MTV that was still showing music videos. Brought into the spotlight by Nine Inch Nails, Marilyn Manson matched the changes that were happening in the culture of the time by upping the visuals & generally being more extreme, disturbing & degenerate than their predecessors. Marilyn Manson was effectively the first Rock Star of Goth/Industrial.

Rob Zombie

Rob Zombie started out in the NYC Punk scene in the 80s playing at places like ABC NO RIO with his band White Zombie (which took their name from a Bela Lugosi movie). His music basically took a Hard Rock/Alternative guitar driven sound & put it on top of electronic dance music with the energy & intention of 80s Punk as its soul. Since launching White Zombie, Rob has released his own movies including a reimagining of John Carpenter's Halloween.

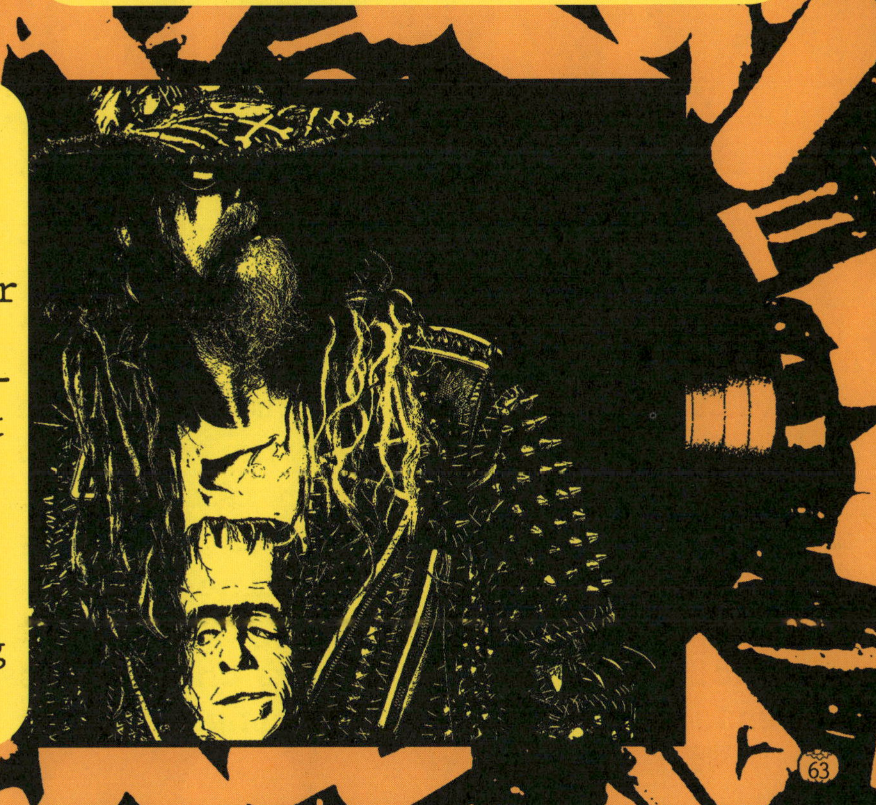

Halloween is Every Day

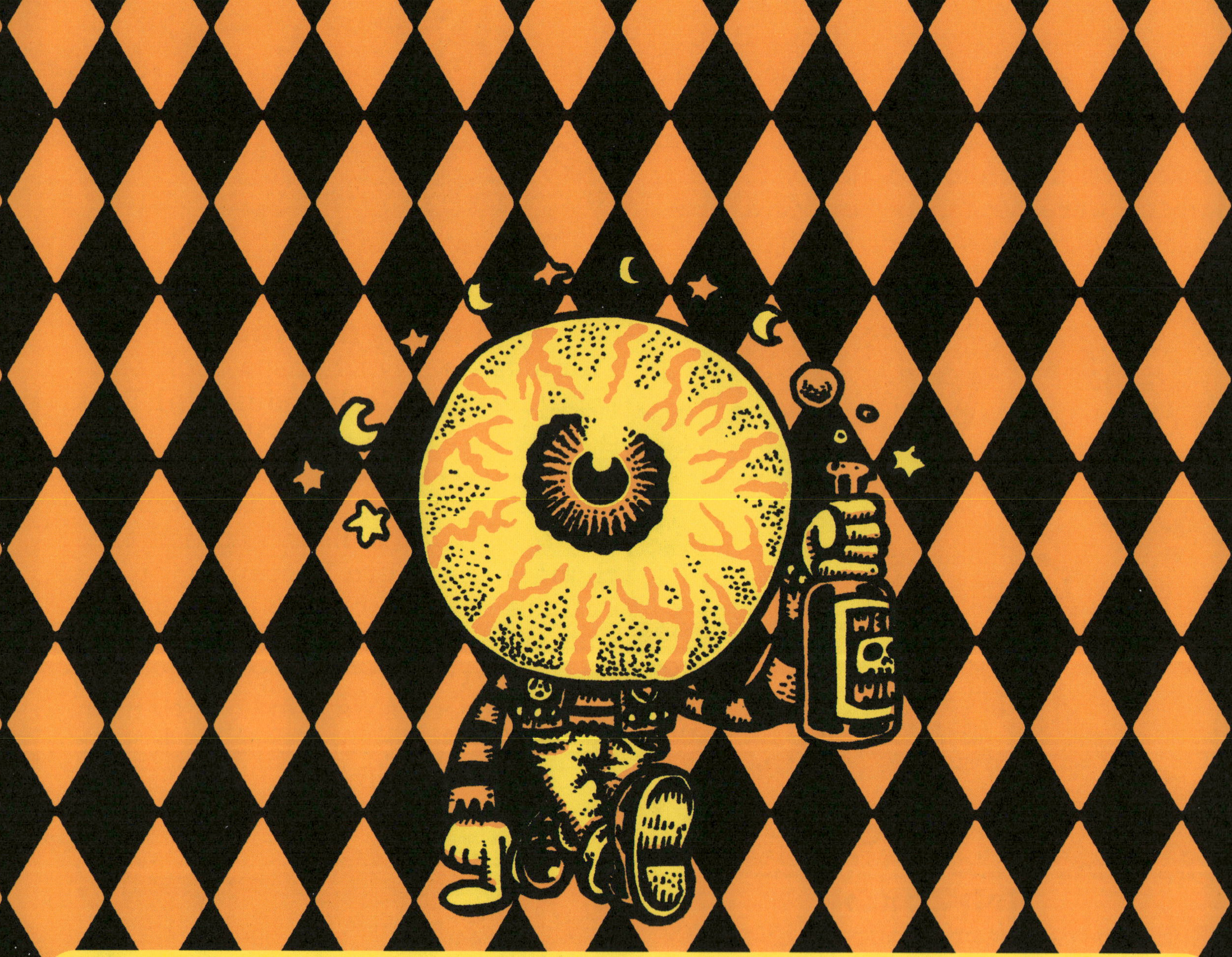

Halloween has come to equate with the noble ideal of "being yourself". Our society has become more permissive in certain ways, but true nonconformist individuals are always looking for a way or excuse to be themselves as they grow up & Halloween fits the bill. I am an individualist & a non-conformist & I love Halloween. I don't need an excuse to be myself. I think being yourself is important for everyone but it also isn't what Halloween is about. "Being Yourself" has any number of results that are as diverse as humanity itself, but Halloween has a definition to it. So, while the line might be "Halloween Is Every Day", what it is actually saying is "be yourself everyday." If the circle is widened it includes the other things that are associated with Halloween, which is especially easy & satisfying if you're on the Gothic end of the spectrum.

Ireally like contrast, so having Halloween year round is a no go for me. I like getting ready for Halloween but I also like putting it away. If you think about it like fasting before a feast, Halloween is the feast of things you love, which is actually strengthened by not being around all year because you are hungry for it! Absence makes the heart grow fonder, but it also strengthens the holiday. Think about it like a hose, where a big aperture keeps the water broad & soft but if you force the water through a small hole, it gets hard & pointed! You are into whatever you're into, but Halloween is a holiday for everyone, once a year. What you must remember is that I am an individualist & a non-conformist but I feel the draw towards guiding the masses. It's a weird & contradictory existence but here we are. What I'm saying is that even though I obviously love Halloween, I also recognize that holidays work better, concentrated & not spread out all over the place.

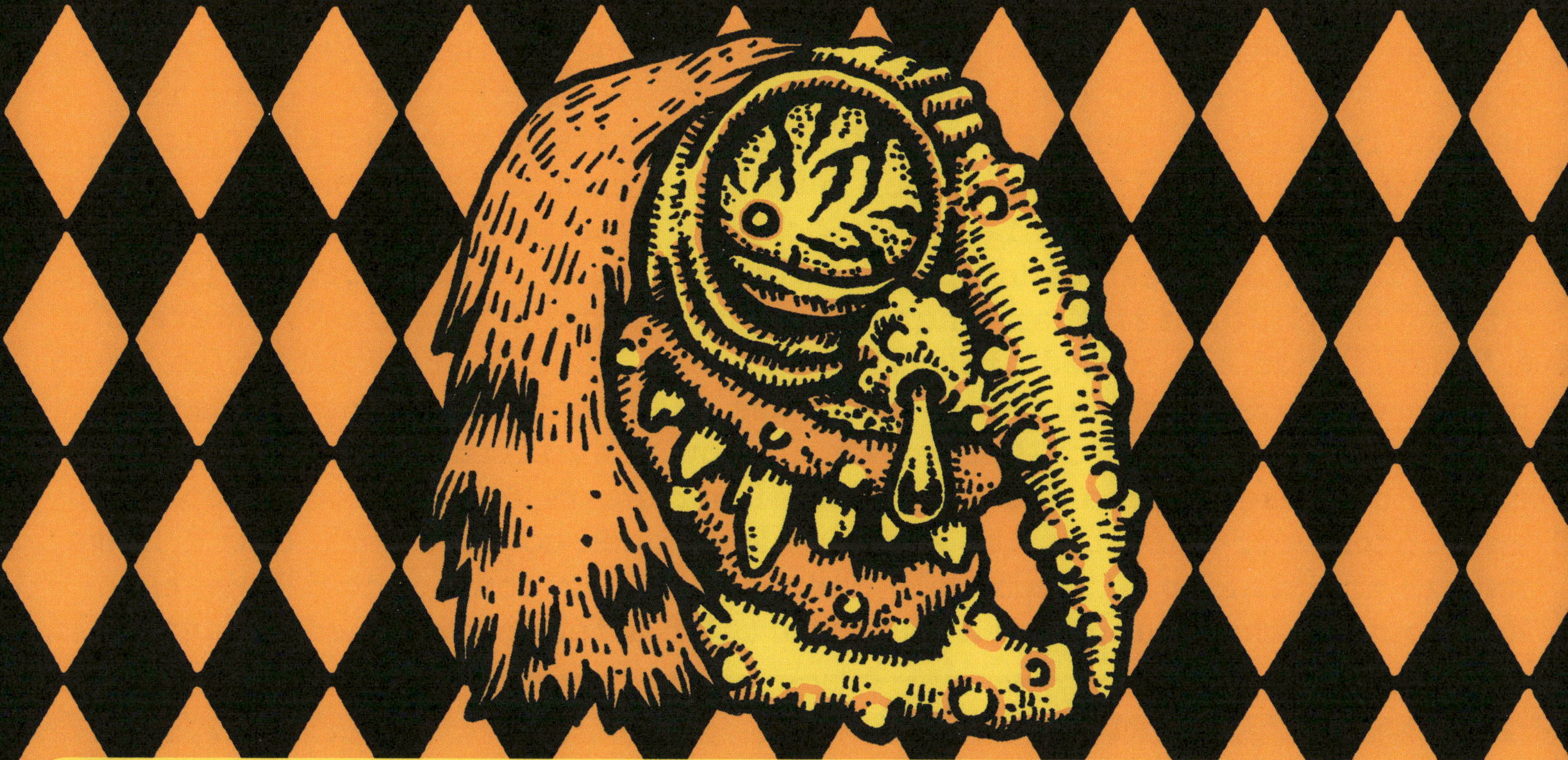

One of the bittersweet realities of life is that it doesn't last forever. That's one of the things you should be thinking about during Halloween. While "I Wanna Rock&Roll All Night & Party Every Day" sounds good, the reality is that if you actually live that way you're guaranteed to burn out if you're lucky & die if you're not. Believe me, I've tried & I know a lot of people that have tried & died. That said, while Halloween Is Every Day is a great song & slogan, it leads to Halloween dilution & a lack of the true energy of putting the correct limitations on this or any holiday. Could you imagine someone who wants Thanksgiving or the 4th of July every day? Just think about it. It's like kids who think they are just going to eat only candy as soon as they have control over their own lives, good luck! Pretty soon you realize that you have to eat your vegetables, hopefully as a child! Also, eating candy only occasionally makes it sweeter & more interesting!

I understand that life can be hard, especially if you're a non-conformist or part of an out-group constantly out of step with the rest of the world. Sometimes, just existing is painful & grating! Because of this it's easy to enter into an adversarial relationship with society & view Halloween as yours & a hidey hole from the rest of humanity, but this isn't the reality of Halloween. Halloween is a holiday for everyone, it has a clear definition & can be enjoyed by all! I wanted to burn society to the ground & dance on the ashes when I was a teenager, partly out of some kind of revenge for feeling damaged as a sensitive, non-conformist child, but over the years I have grown, healed & changed my view on society. We have to give Halloween to everyone to help heal this broken world. Society will change, especially if we show that we are invested. If you look at the amount of bullying that people put up with & dish out today it's so much smaller than when I was growing up! The world has changed, so much of the old way was developed as a defense mechanism against threats that no longer exist! Yes, there are new threats & peoples & places that are not even approaching this level of progress, but i'm centrally talking about the USA & the west here. It's very difficult to put down your shield because you have been shot with arrows for so long, but that is what I'm asking you to do! Flip over your shield & turn it into a Trick or Treat candy bowl! It is very easy to turn people into the "other" & dehumanize them, there's language around "normies" & "Karens" & "Chads" that are tossed around tons lately. I think it is better to treat people on an individual level & not use these dehumanizing terms, but allow people to stand on their own. I know it's difficult to not categorize & dehumanize the sheer number of strangers & obnoxious people we encounter every day, but it's something we need to do. I don't think human nature is going to miraculously change but I am confident & have seen how society can change with the efforts of a few determined individuals.

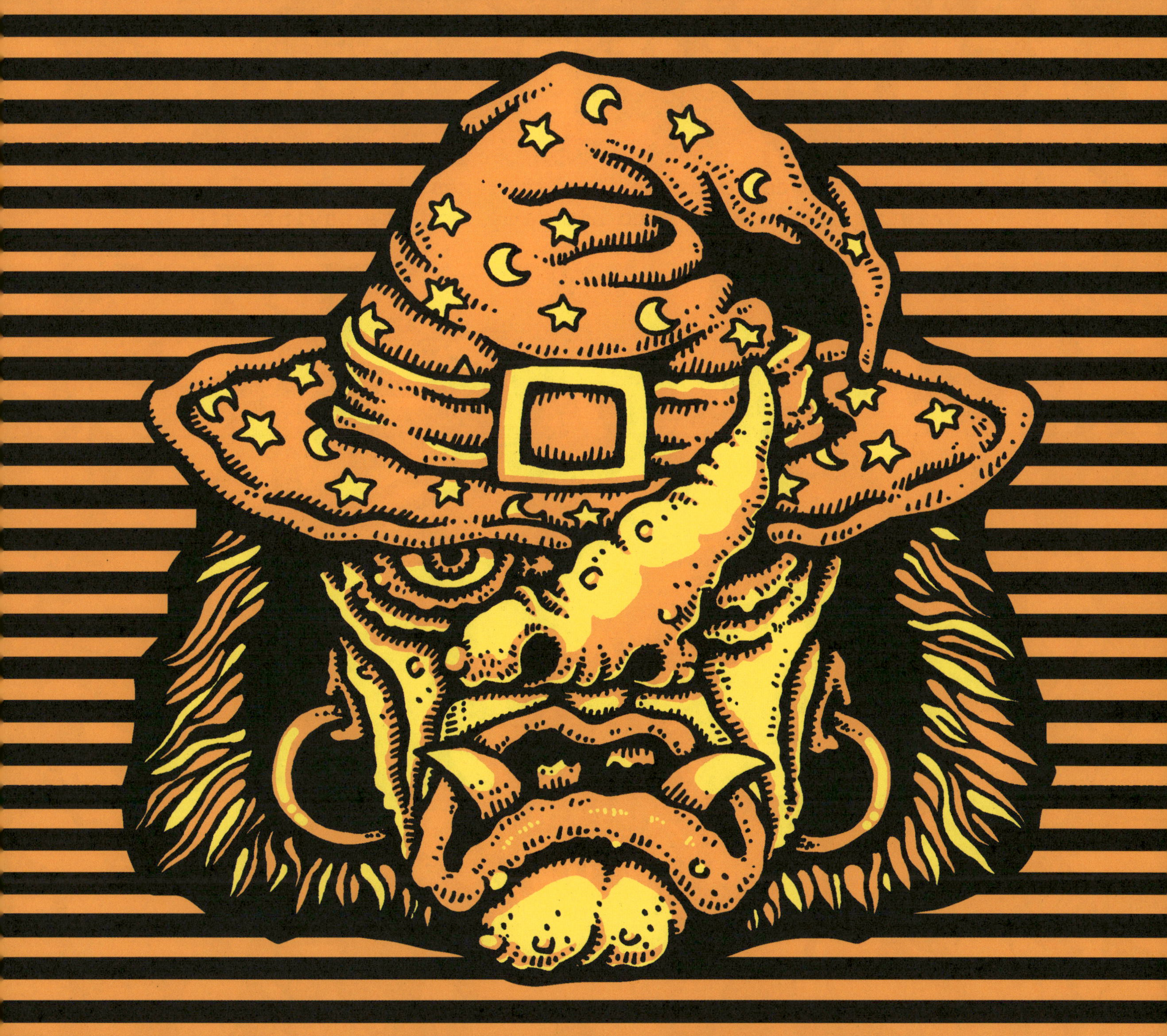

e who love Halloween don't have that far to go to get this holi- day really strong. We need to stop clutching Halloween so hard & let it run wild! In some ways this is a metaphysical mission, where the "letting go" of Halloween transfers that subcultural energy it has into broad cultural energy that can spread among the people. I know that so- ciety is at a particularly low-point; fragmented, reactionary & calcified right now, but it is important to remember that society is always there. In a similarly metaphysical strategy, the hardness of society right now can be softened by fluidity. So, all in all I'm saying that "Every Day Is Halloween" is a bad idea, but I agree with the sentiment. It makes Hallow- een stronger to have it be on one day.

Anti Halloween

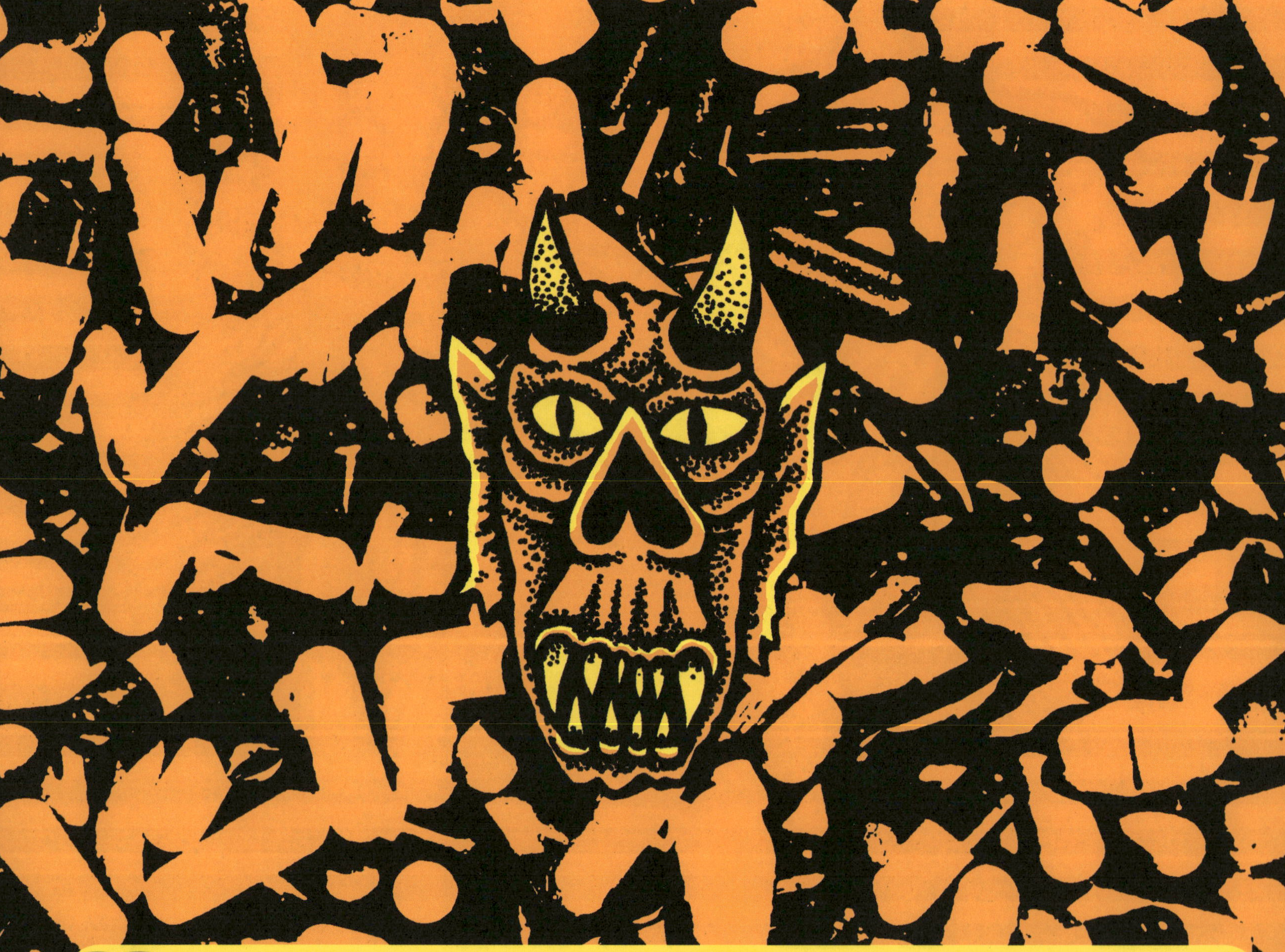

Halloween is a natural thorn in the side of control-freaks. Whether this is Christian fundamentalists, concerned parents, the politically correct or the chaos-vampiric news media that feeds into their madness, this holiday is troublesome! Control is a delusion, we have no hope of control over this world. Halloween is accepting of this fact & maybe even celebrates it! That said, it is not wise to court this kind of chaos constantly. Your life needs a certain kind of order, but it also needs a steam valve so it doesn't get too rigid, this is the function of Halloween. Still, there are people that are so obsessed with control that they are existentially threatened by Halloween & they are always piping up about why Halloween is bad. These people are so easy to irritate, it's difficult not to play along. But, my strategy as of late has been not to.

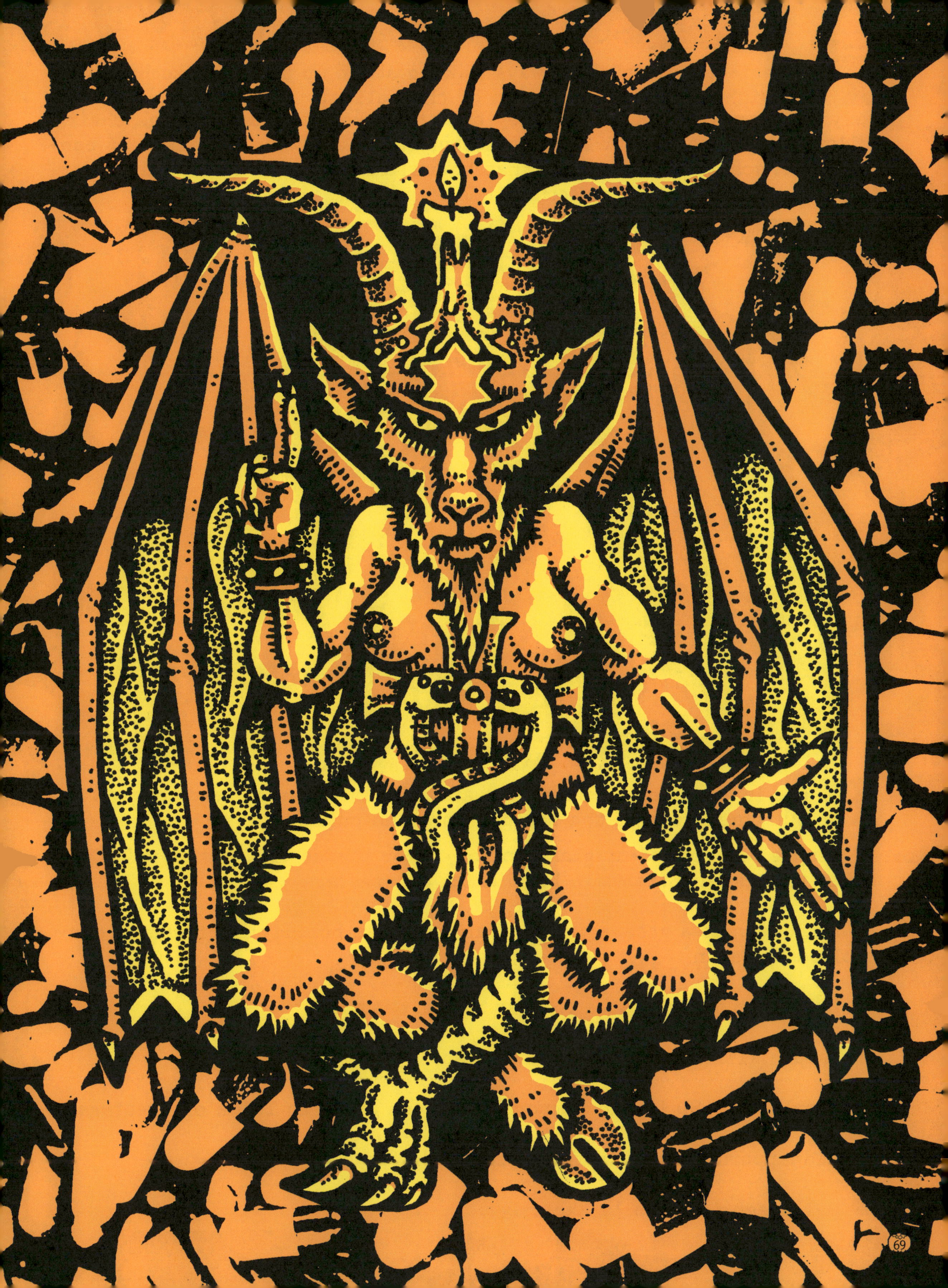

The anti-Halloween are always making stuff up to demonize Halloween with their base. The core of the holiday is already accepted & very popular with society so they have to make stuff up to shock their followers into action. We already accept that Halloween is a time of controlled chaos & morbidity, but that annual reminder of death & disorder is very uncomfortable for some kinds of people.

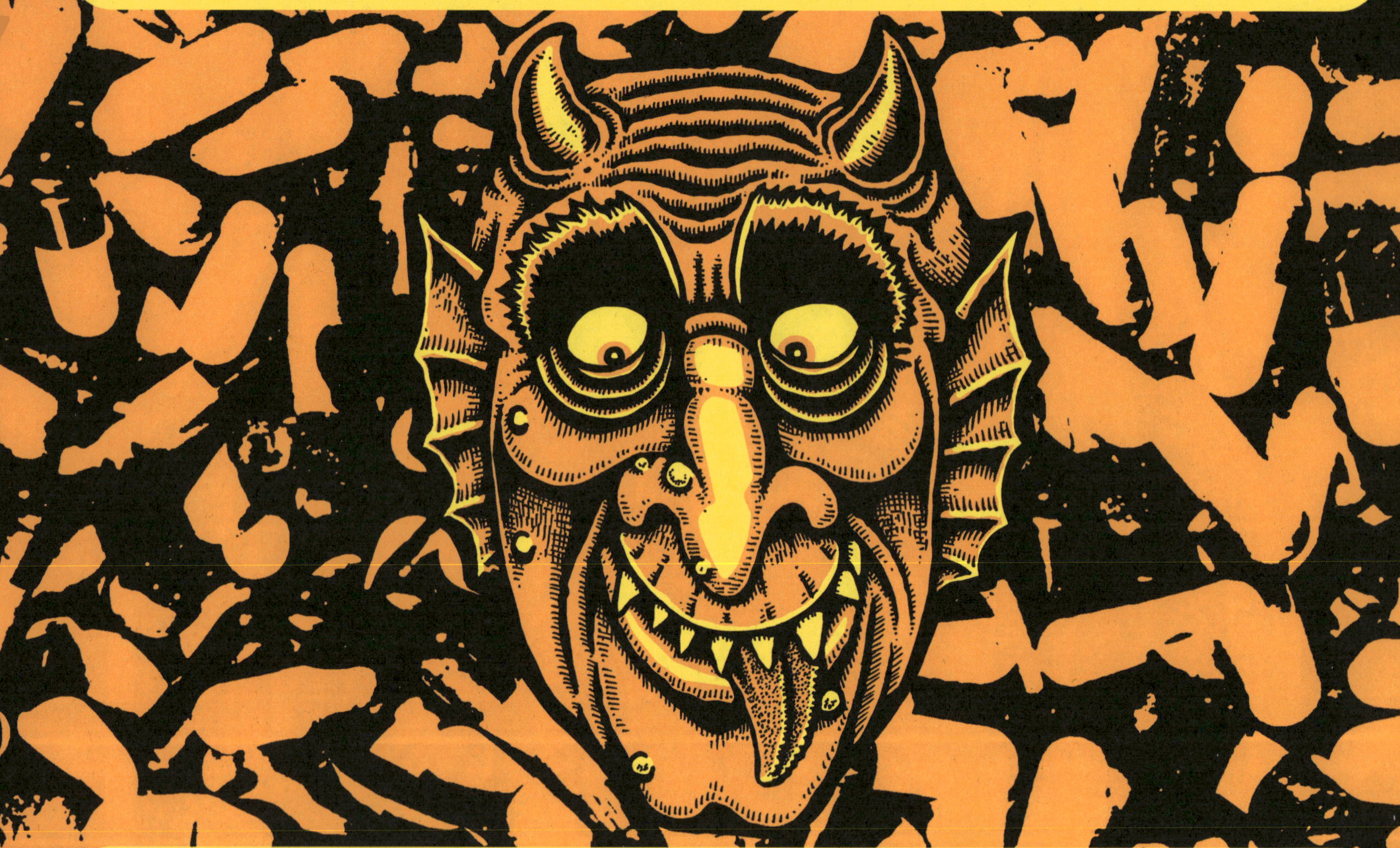

Here is a list of lies that the anti-Halloween have used to try to put their fear of the holiday into the public.

🎃 People put ground-up glass, poison, razor blades, LSD, Anthrax, THC & other things into treats to harm trick or treaters.

🎃 Halloween is a gateway into Satanism & the holiday is created & controlled by Satan.

🎃 Halloween is an excuse to wear racist costumes.

🎃 People kill black cats on Halloween.

🎃 People put LSD in the temporary tattoos given to Trick or Treaters.

🎃 Kidnappers are out in full-force on Halloween.

🎃 Halloween is racially exclusive.

Society just has certain moral-panics that arise in different times. If you are cool-headed these are things you just have to learn to live with, if you succumb to panic, you get swept up in the latest craze. It's difficult because the people get obsessed with the panic, the media takes note & feeds into the panic to seem more human & then even more people are panicking! I'm not saying that there aren't plenty of reasons to panic, what I'm saying is that panicking as a response is not good, no matter what. The problem is that most people that are caught up in a panic don't realize they are caught up in a panic!

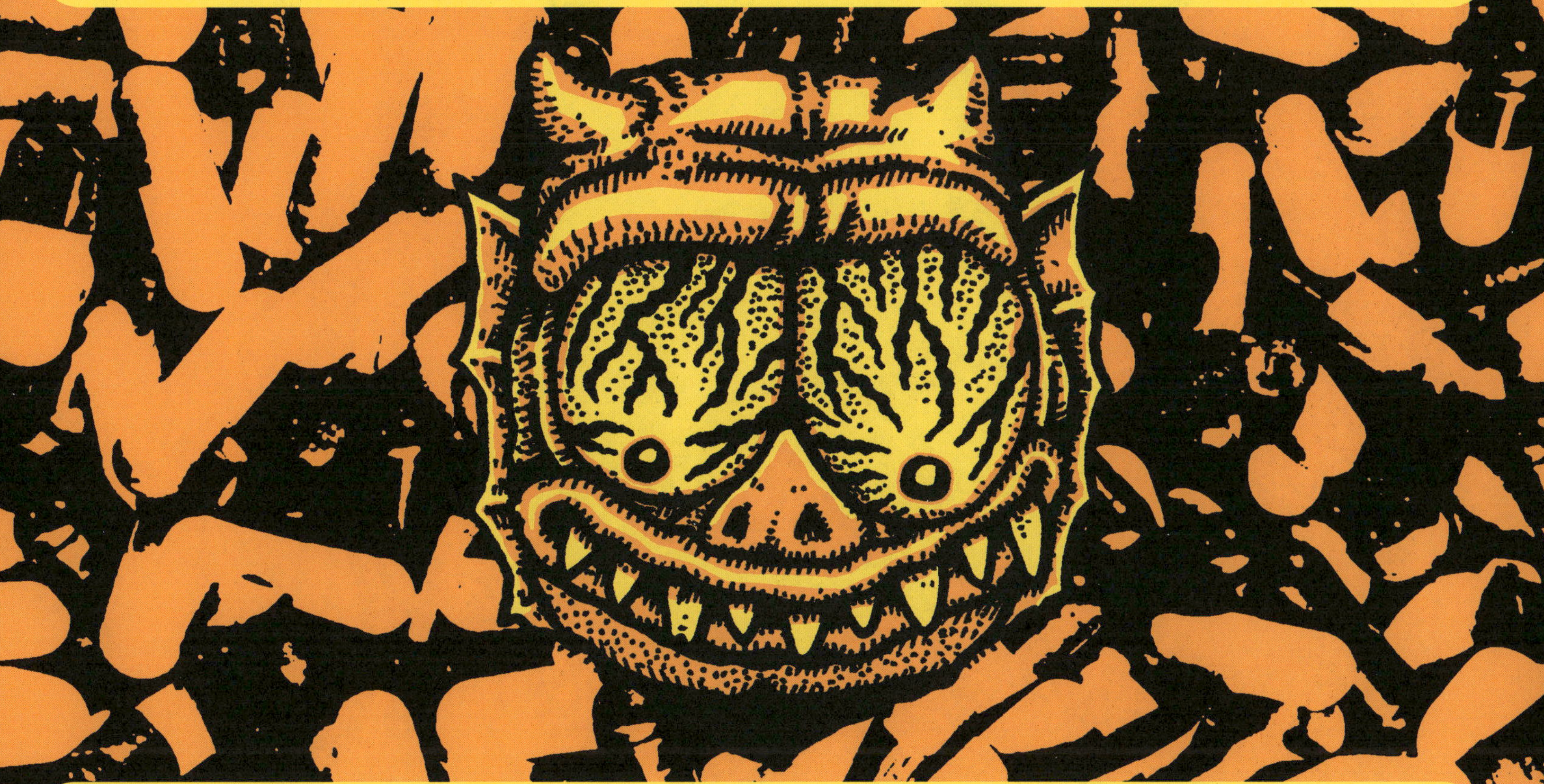

Don't panic! I've provided a list to help see or if you or the people around you have gotten swept up in a panic!

- Fear of dying or fear of others dying.
- Fear of losing control.
- Feelings of detachment.
- Desire to cut-off people who aren't panicking also.
- Projecting your fears onto people less powerful than you.
- You spend sleepless hours at night obsessing over your issue.
- A desire for total control without accountability.
- No tolerance for questions or critical inquiry.
- You feel like you can never be good enough.
- Fear about the outside world, such as catastrophes & conspiracies.
- Desire for easy solutions.

If you feel yourself getting swept up in a panic it is good to do some breathing exercises, diversify your media intake & your friend group, limit your social media consumption & consumption of sugar & caffeine.

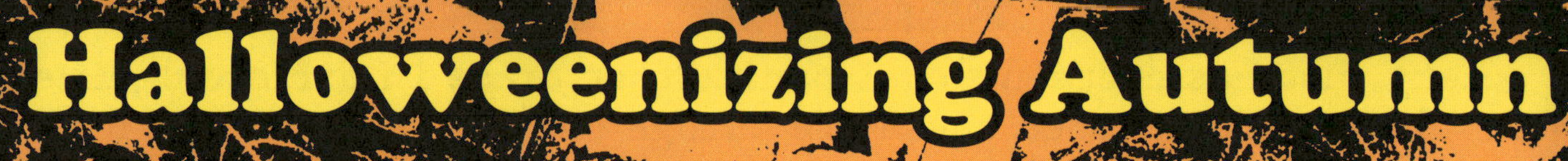

Halloweenizing Autumn

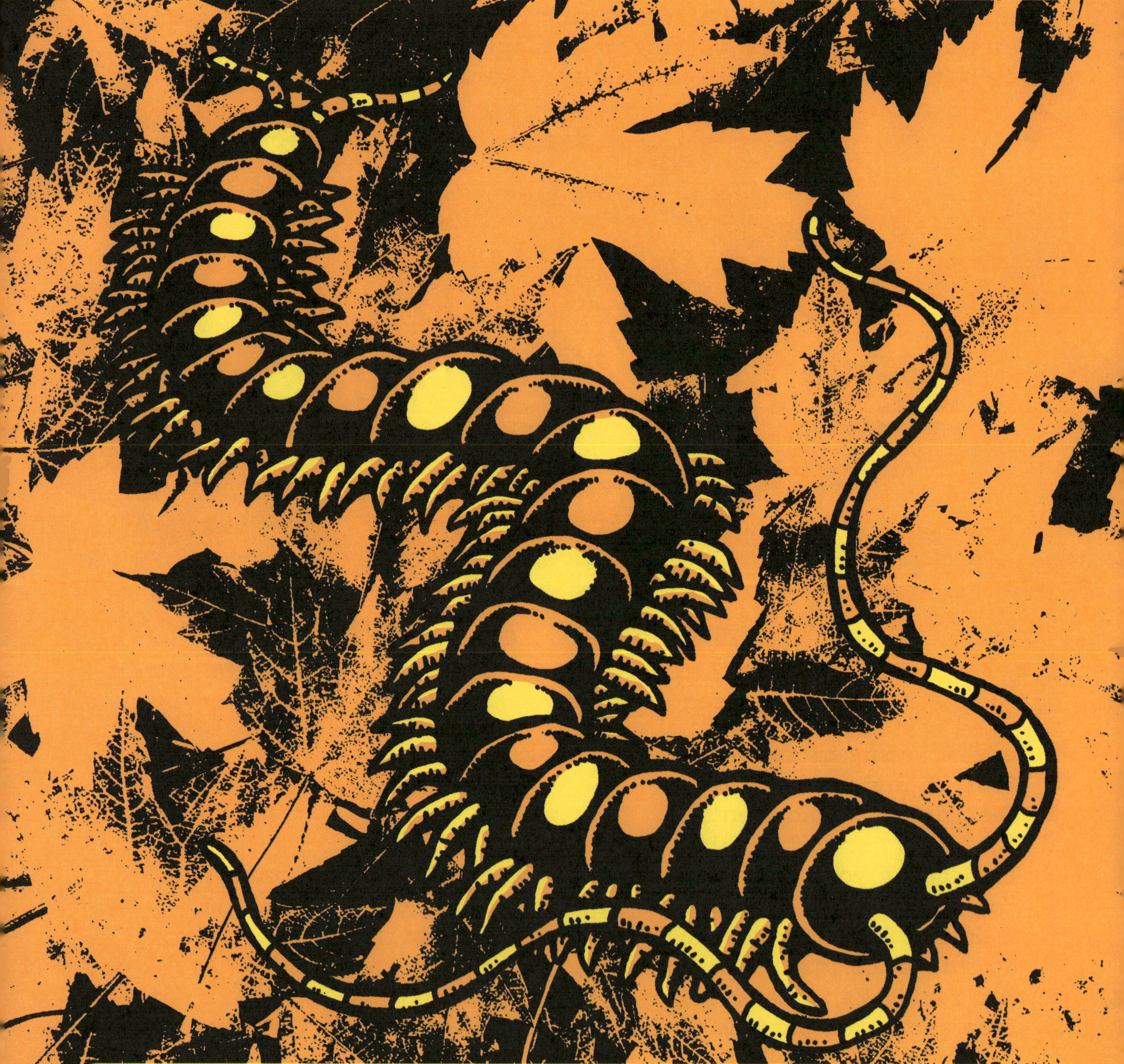

Autumn is a three month season & you can see Halloween as its crown. There is obviously Thanksgiving in there, but Thanksgiving has this heavy colonial weight to it, that makes it less universal than Halloween. Because of this I advocate for the Halloweenification of Fall.

Autumn brings us the return to school & all the drudgery that entails… but also there is a distinct character to the season that Halloween plays off of. In Autumn, the sun is out for a shorter time, the earth dries out, the leaves change color & fall from the trees, the animals gather food for winter & the mornings & evenings begin to get a nip of cold on them & you begin to see your breath. The cawing of crows takes on a different character in this time of year, they are harbingers of Halloween. This is the time for spiced apple cider & hot chocolate with marshmallows & walks through the park to see the mushrooms starting to appear. I find it very rewarding to see the leaves changing colors at this time of year, it's a nice thing to appreciate, a reminder of the changing seasons & if you want to go there, the impending death that occurs in Winter. All of your Autumn decorating doesn't have to use the outwardly supernatural elements of Halloween, you can mix it up. Use overtly Autumn motifs in your Halloween decorating & then after Halloween passes you can take the supernatural & death themed decorations down & leave up the Fall decorations until after Thanksgiving. All the pumpkins, leaves, spider webs, scarecrows & stuff like that can stay up & lend their flavor to the season! I feel like this approach can also breath new life into Thanksgiving, especially for people who have ideological problems with the holiday. Let Halloween overshadow & flavor Thanksgiving & all of Fall, the season demands it, the season needs seasoning! Add pumpkin spice!

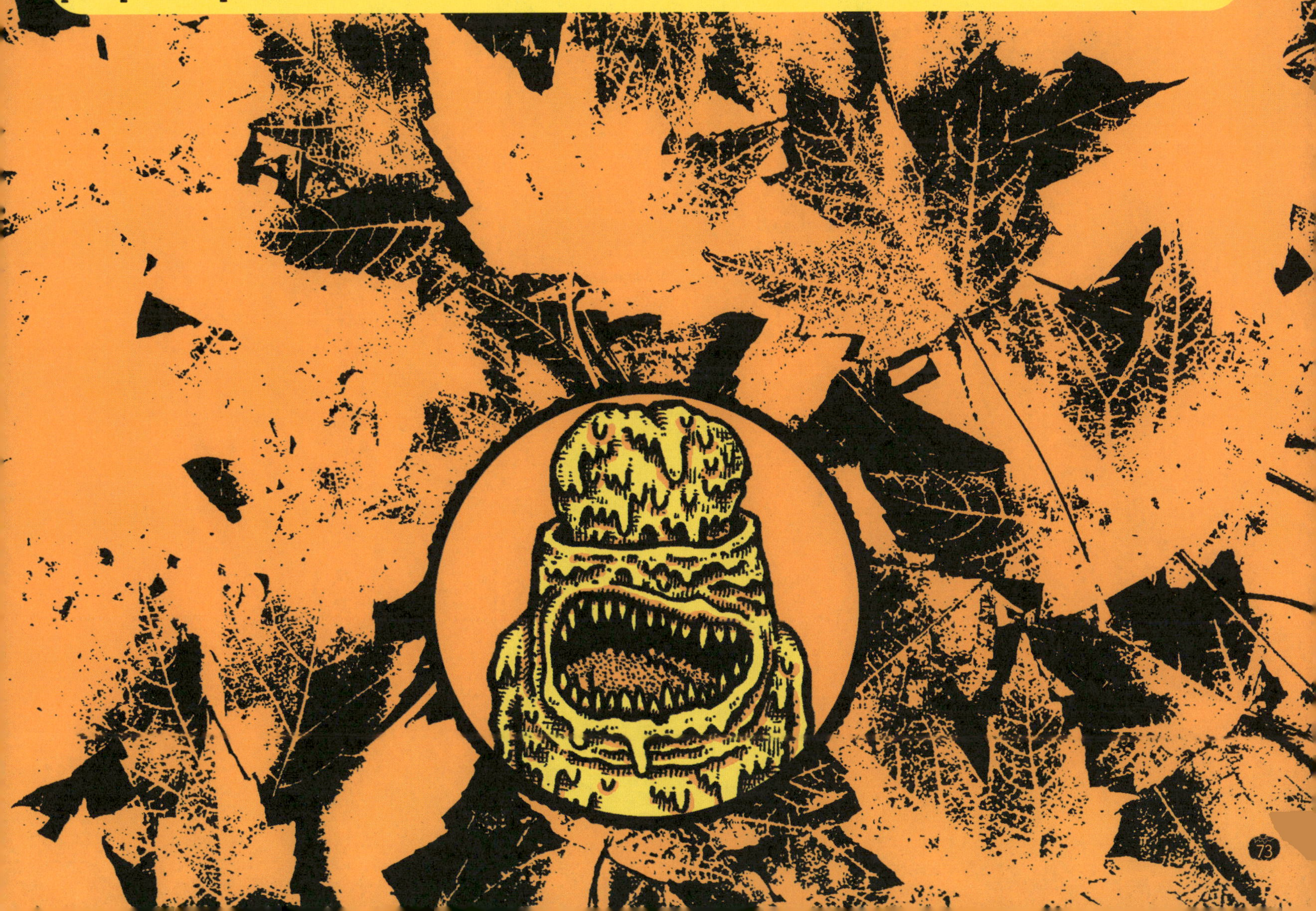

We don't have to go by how the seasons or anything have been defined before us, we can redefine them based on utility, natural reality & how we'd like them to be. This is at the core of my desires for Halloween & for my desires for everything. So we don't have to let Autumn be defined by back to school & we don't have to let Thanksgiving be charaterised by some ignorant, propagandistic view of history. We can have Autumn be defined by something we love, it can be defined by Halloween! As we live in the chaos & fluidity of the present moment we are being given an opportunity to do things how we want to, not as a reaction to the past or as defined by other people. In this moment & all moments it is very important to look at things as clearly as possible & base our actions on this clarity. Our approach to Autumn should be in this way, looking at the reality of the season & giving it flavor from what we like. I went from being a "Halloween is Every Day" guy to being a "Halloweenizing Autumn" guy. Every season has its perks, & they deserve to shine on their own. I grew up in Oakland, California which basically has one long season & now I live in Portland, Oregon where there are four distinct seasons & I dig it. I also just have worked really hard to separate my emotional feelings about being myself from Halloween. I am just myself all year long & keep the Halloween stuff to Autumn.

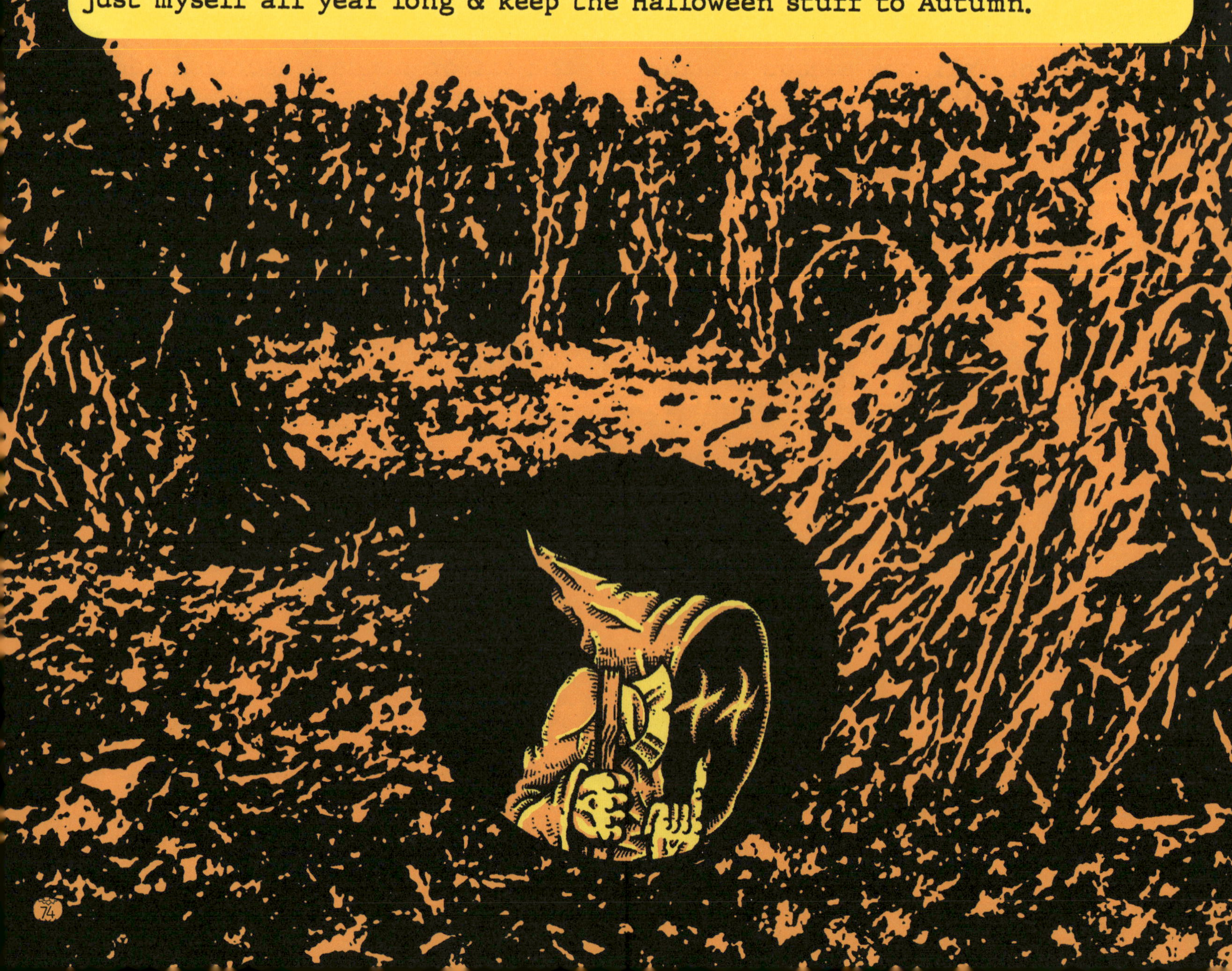

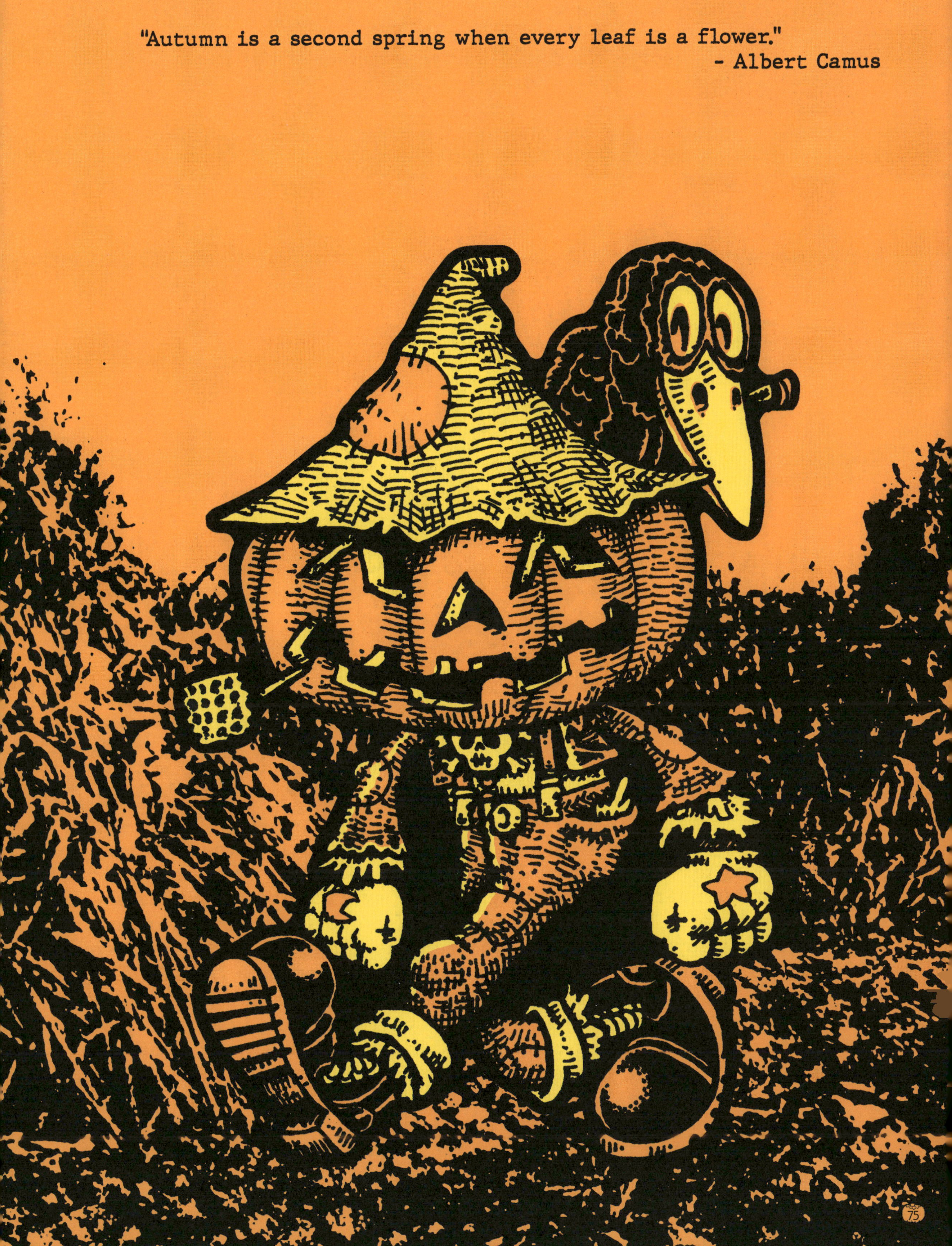

"Autumn is a second spring when every leaf is a flower."
- Albert Camus

In Conclusion

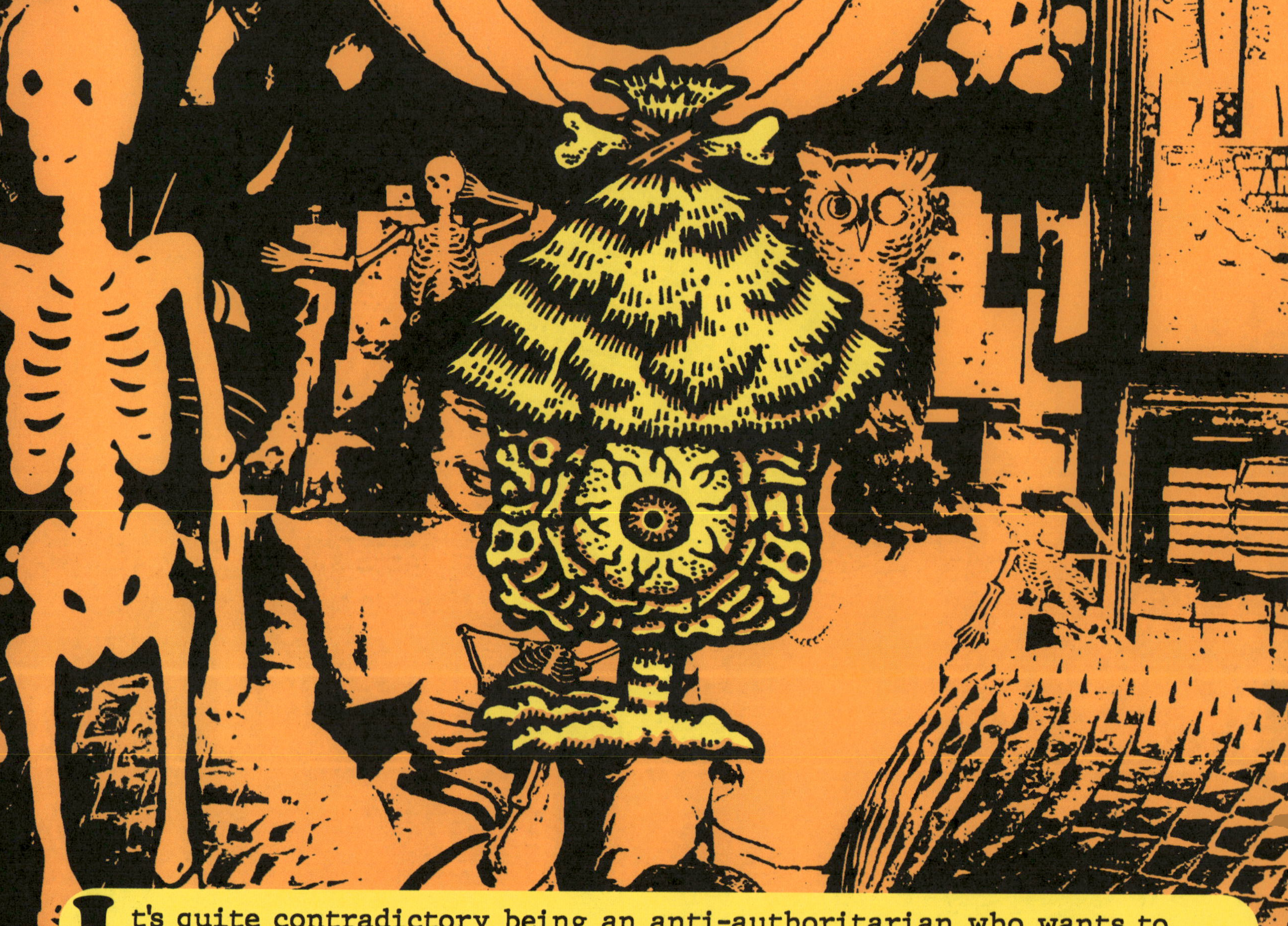

It's quite contradictory being an anti-authoritarian who wants to make rules for society to follow. How are the rules enforced? I find it a similar quandary as parenting, I know my kids are individuals with their own destinies but at the same time, i've got some desire for how their lives are supposed to go & expectations about certain hopes I've got. That said, I think the healthiest way to manage this is talk it over & express my desires. This book details my desires for Halloween, it uses concrete examples to make the point, but ultimately it is about my vision for the holiday. My desire to make things a certain way comes from a utilitarian approach, where I see a use for these things & ultimately a benefit to the people. The problem is we live in a system that seems to say yes a lot, but I think this is because the right questions aren't being asked. My angle is to say yes & no, because you need both options working together to define reality.

The best way to effect change is to lead by example & always remember the Golden Rule 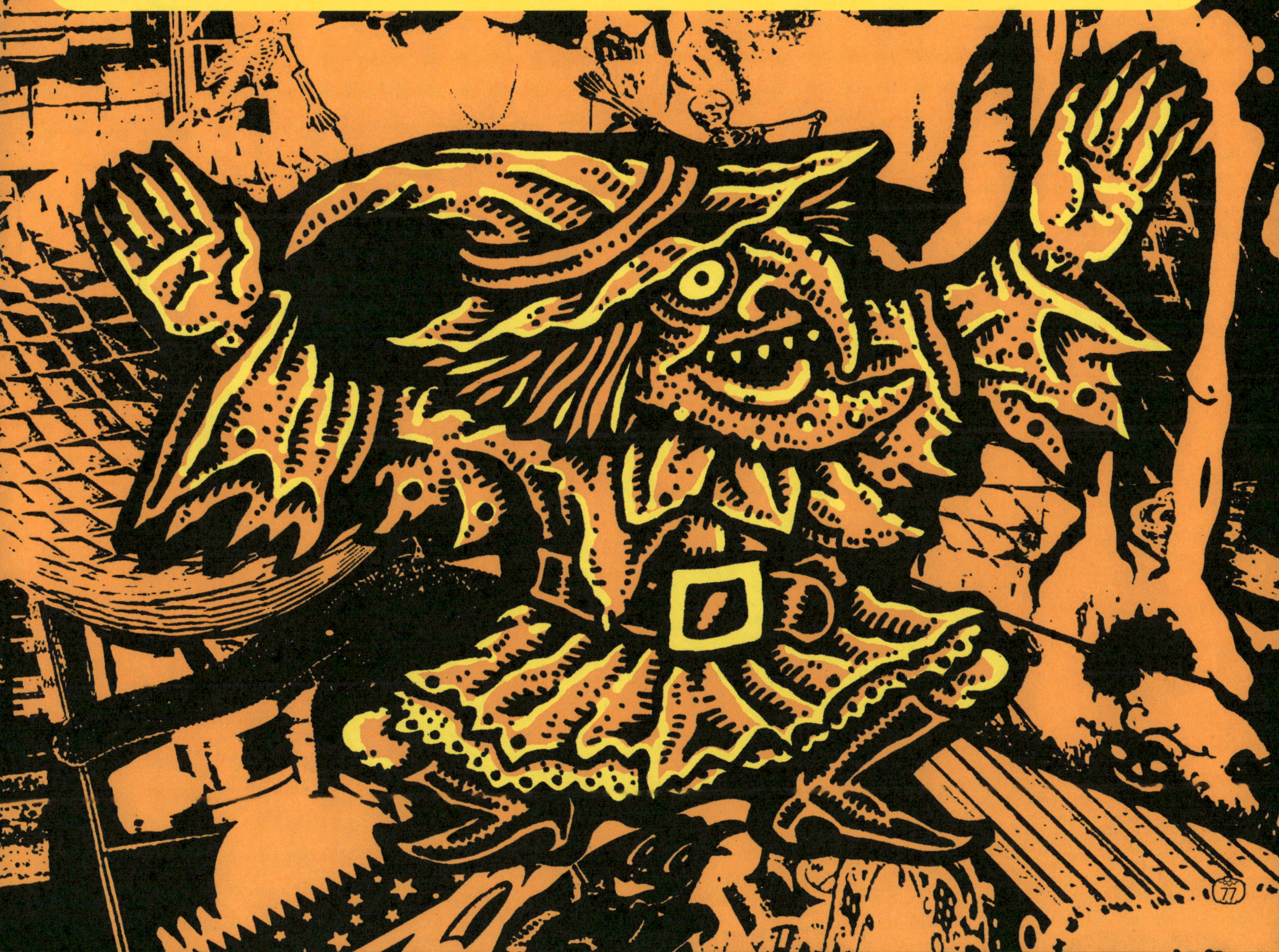. Remember that change is rarely instantaneous & usually goes at a snail's pace so you have to be patient. There will inevitably be set-backs & bumps in the road! You might not even be able to see the change in your lifetime, you've got to take the historical longview! People will inevitably copy what works & ignore what doesn't. They just have to see the thing. You can effect change using force but it operates like a rubber band, reality can be pushed a direction, but eventually it snaps back & then returns to its natural state. Wronged people will hold a grudge stubbornly & even generationally. I acknowledge that there is a certain unnatural quality to culture & this is some of what separates us from the other animals, but culture is the primary area that I'm focused on. I am positive that we love & create culture naturally. Put humanity isolated somewhere & they will just start making stuff up. People just love this stuff, they need it. I know that a better & more relevant Halloween will scratch people's itches harder & just be more satisfying to them!

That's "Do unto others as you would have them do unto you." It's unfortunate that I feel we need to repeat such basic moral lessons, but that's where we're at.

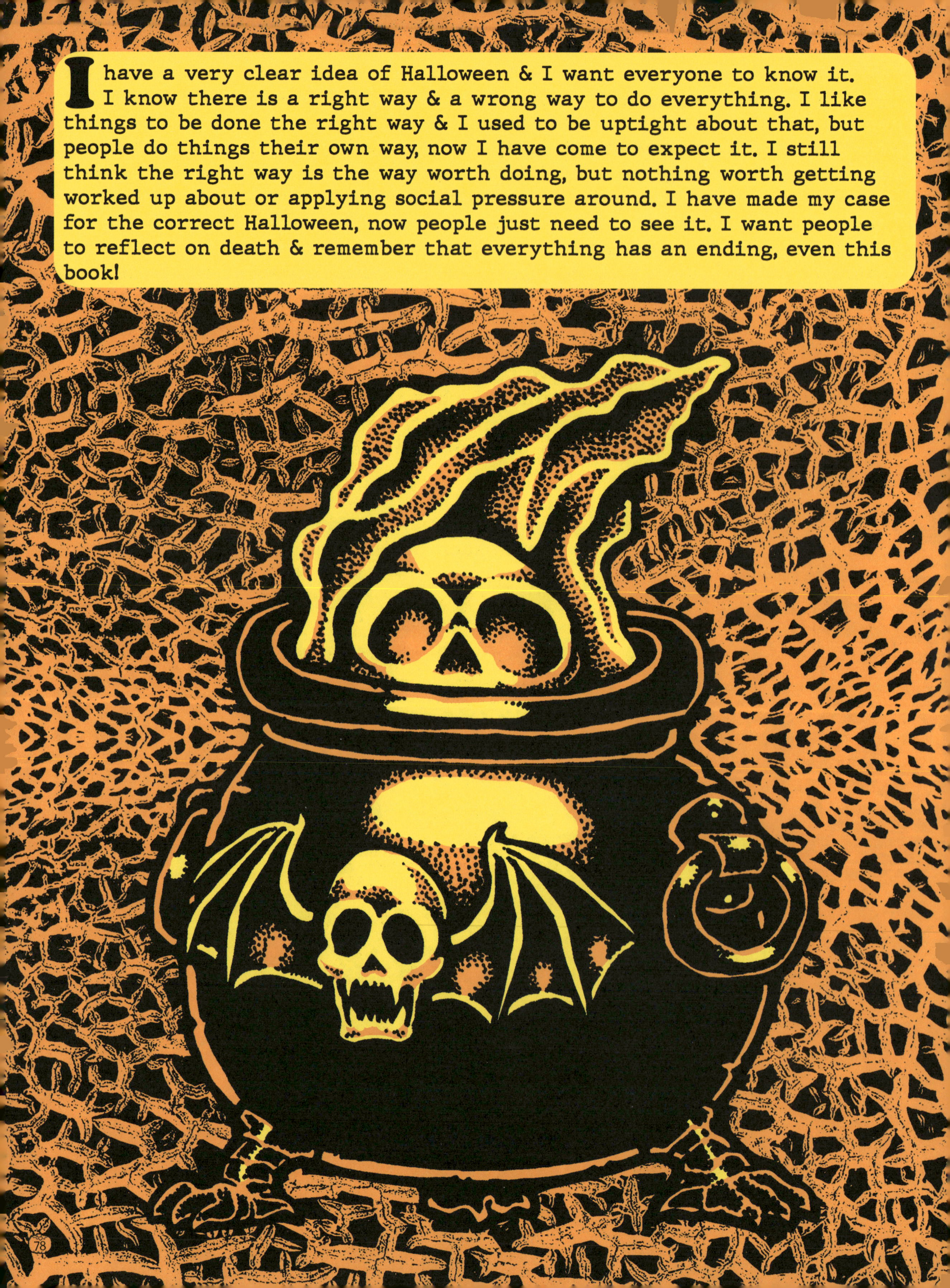

I have a very clear idea of Halloween & I want everyone to know it. I know there is a right way & a wrong way to do everything. I like things to be done the right way & I used to be uptight about that, but people do things their own way, now I have come to expect it. I still think the right way is the way worth doing, but nothing worth getting worked up about or applying social pressure around. I have made my case for the correct Halloween, now people just need to see it. I want people to reflect on death & remember that everything has an ending, even this book!

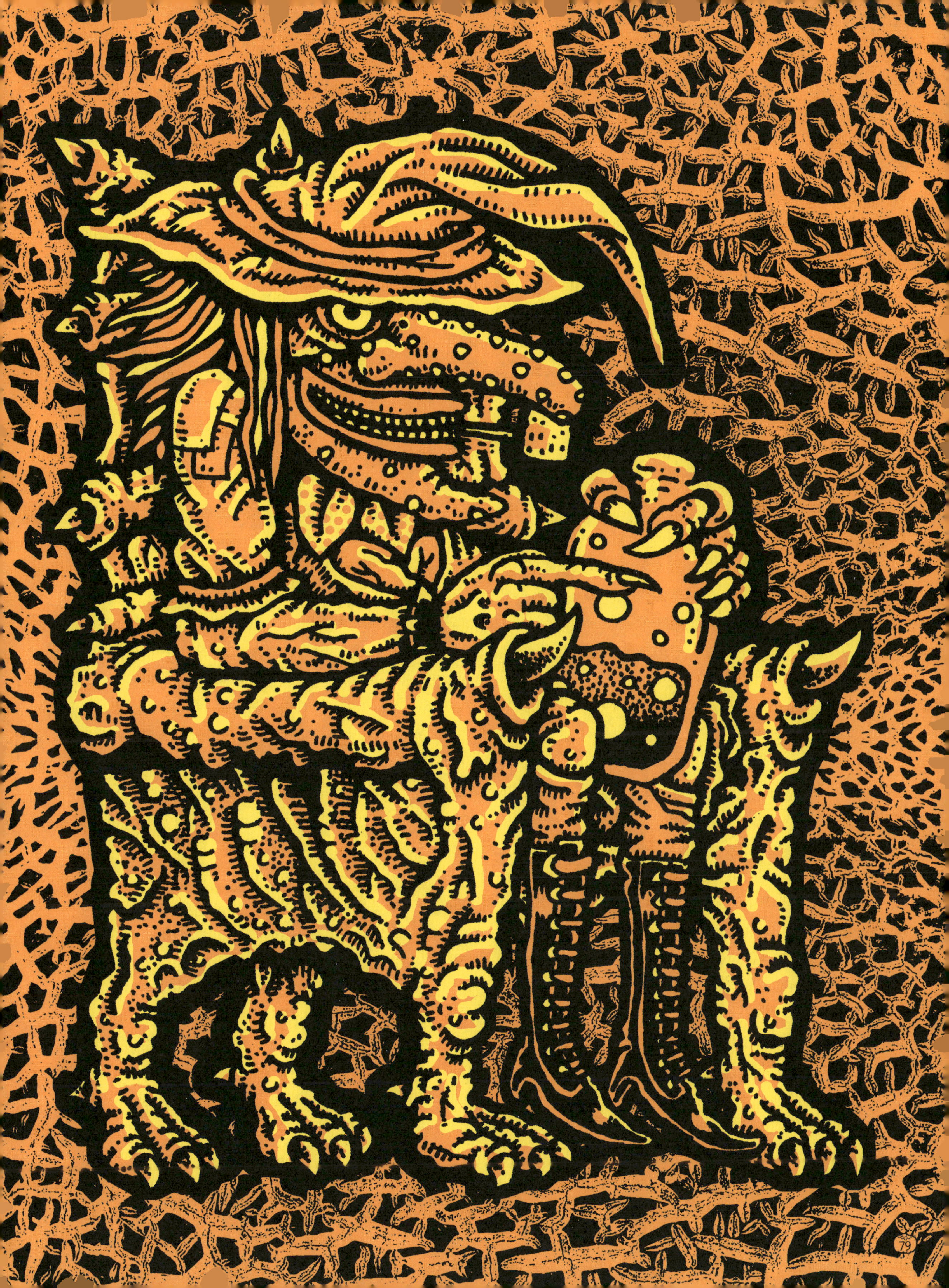